GREEN HILLS OF AFRICA

BOOKS BY ERNEST HEMINGWAY

CHARLES SCRIBNER'S SONS

GREEN HILLS OF AFRICA

By

ERNEST HEMINGWAY

Decorations by EDWARD SHENTON

CHARLES SCRIBNER'S SONS, NEW YORK

TO PHILIP, TO CHARLES,
AND TO SULLY

FOREWORD

Unlike many novels, none of the characters or incidents in this book is imaginary. Any one not finding sufficient love interest is at liberty, while reading it, to insert whatever love interest he or she may have at the time. The writer has attempted to write an absolutely true book to see whether the shape of a country and the pattern of a month's action can, if truly presented, compete with a work of the imagination.

GREEN HILLS OF AFRICA

PART I

Pursuit and Conversation

CHAPTER

WE were sitting in the blind that Wanderobo hunters had built of twigs and branches at the edge of the salt-lick when we heard the truck coming. At first it was far away and no one could tell what the noise was. Then it was stopped and we hoped it had been nothing or perhaps only the wind. Then it moved slowly nearer, unmistakable now, louder and louder until, agonizing in a clank of loud irregular explosions, it passed close behind us to go on up the road. The theatrical one of the two trackers stood up.

"It is finished," he said.

ONE

I put my hand to my mouth and motioned him down.

"It is finished," he said again and spread his arms wide. I had never liked him and I liked him less now.

"After," I whispered. M'Cola shook his head. I looked at his bald black skull and he turned his face a little so that I saw the thin Chinese hairs at the corners of his mouth.

"No good," he said. *"Hapana m'uzuri."*

"Wait a little," I told him. He bent his head down again so that it would not show above the dead branches and we sat there in the dust of the hole until it was too dark to see the front sight on my rifle; but nothing more came. The theatrical tracker was impatient and restless. A little before the last of the light was gone he whispered to M'Cola that it was now too dark to shoot.

"Shut up, you," M'Cola told him. "The Bwana can shoot after you cannot see."

The other tracker, the educated one, gave another demonstration of his education by scratching his name, Abdullah, on the black skin of his leg with a sharp twig. I watched without admiration and M'Cola looked at the word without a shadow of expression on his face. After a while the tracker scratched it out.

Finally I made a last sight against what was left of the light and saw it was no use, even with the large aperture.

M'Cola was watching.

"No good," I said.

"Yes," he agreed, in Swahili. "Go to camp?"

"Yes."

We stood up and made our way out of the blind and out through the trees, walking on the sandy loam, feeling our way between trees and under branches, back to the road. A mile along the road was the car. As we came alongside, Kamau, the driver, put the lights on.

The truck had spoiled it. That afternoon we had left the car up the road and approached the salt-lick very carefully. There had been a little rain, the day before, though not enough to flood the lick, which was simply an

4

opening in the trees with a patch of earth worn into deep circles and grooved at the edges with hollows where the animals had licked the dirt for salt, and we had seen long, heart-shaped, fresh tracks of four greater kudu bulls that had been on the salt the night before, as well as many newly pressed tracks of lesser kudu. There was also a rhino who, from the tracks and the kicked-up mound of strawy dung, came there each night. The blind had been built at close arrow-shot of the lick and sitting, leaning back, knees high, heads low, in a hollow half full of ashes and dust, watching through the dried leaves and thin branches I had seen a lesser kudu bull come out of the brush to the edge of the opening where the salt was and stand there, heavy-necked, gray, and handsome, the horns spiralled against the sun while I sighted on his chest and then refused the shot, wanting not to frighten the greater kudu that should surely come at dusk. But before we ever heard the truck the bull had heard it and run off into the trees and everything else that had been moving, in the bush on the flats, or coming down from the small hills through the trees, coming toward the salt, had halted at that exploding, clanking sound. They would come, later, in the dark; but then it would be too late.

So now, going along the sandy track of the road in the car, the lights picking out the eyes of night birds that squatted close on the sand until the bulk of the car was on them and they rose in soft panic; passing the fires of the travellers that all moved to the westward by day along this road, abandoning the famine country that was ahead of us; me sitting, the butt of my rifle on my foot, the barrel in the crook of my left arm, a flask of whiskey between my knees, pouring the whiskey into a tin cup and passing it over my shoulder in the dark for M'Cola to pour water into it from the canteen, drinking this, the first one of the day, the finest one there is, and looking at the thick bush we passed in the dark, feeling the cool wind of the night and smelling the good smell of Africa, I was altogether happy.

Then ahead we saw a big fire and as we came up and passed, I made out a truck beside the road. I told Kamau to stop and go back and as we backed into the firelight there was a short, bandy-legged man with a Tyroler hat, leather shorts, and an open shirt standing before an un-hooded engine in a crowd of natives.

"Can we help?" I asked him.

"No," he said. "Unless you are a mechanic. It has taken a dislike to me. All engines dislike me."

"Do you think it could be the timer? It sounded as though it might be a timing knock when you went past us."

"I think it is much worse than that. It sounds to be something very bad."

"If you can get to our camp we have a mechanic."

"How far is it?"

"About twenty miles."

"In the morning I will try it. Now I am afraid to

make it go farther with that noise of death inside. It is trying to die because it dislikes me. Well, I dislike it too. But if I die it would not annoy it."

"Will you have a drink?" I held out the flask. "Hemingway is my name."

"Kandisky," he said and bowed. "Hemingway is a name I have heard. Where? Where have I heard it? Oh, yes. The *dichter*. You know Hemingway the poet?"

"Where did you read him?"

"In the *Querschnitt*."

"That is me," I said, very pleased. The *Querschnitt* was a German magazine I had written some rather obscene poems for, and published a long story in, years before I could sell anything in America.

"This is very strange," the man in the Tyroler hat said. "Tell me, what do you think of Ringelnatz?"

"He is splendid."

"So. You like Ringelnatz. Good. What do you think of Heinrich Mann?"

"He is no good."

"You believe it?"

"All I know is that I cannot read him."

"He is no good at all. I see we have things in common. What are you doing here?"

"Shooting."

"Not ivory, I hope."

"No. For kudu."

7

"Why should any man shoot a kudu? You, an intelligent man, a poet, to shoot kudu."

"I haven't shot any yet," I said. "But we've been hunting them hard now for ten days. We would have got one tonight if it hadn't been for your lorry."

"That poor lorry. But you should hunt for a year. At the end of that time you have shot everything and you are sorry for it. To hunt for one special animal is nonsense. Why do you do it?"

"I like to do it."

"Of course, if you *like* to do it. Tell me, what do you really think of Rilke?"

"I have read only the one thing."

"Which?"

"The Cornet."

"You liked it?"

"Yes."

"I have no patience with it. It is snobbery. Valery, yes. I see the point of Valery; although there is much snobbery too. Well at least you do not kill elephants."

"I'd kill a big enough one."

"How big?"

"A seventy pounder. Maybe smaller."

"I see there are things we do not agree on. But it is a pleasure to meet one of the great old *Querschnitt* group. Tell me what is Joyce like? I have not the money to buy it. Sinclair Lewis is nothing. I bought it. No. No. Tell me tomorrow. You do not mind if I am camped

8

near? You are with friends? You have a white hunter?"

"With my wife. We would be delighted. Yes, a white hunter."

"Why is he not out with you?"

"He believes you should hunt kudu alone."

"It is better not to hunt them at all. What is he? English?"

"Yes."

"Bloody English?"

"No. Very nice. You will like him."

"You must go. I must not keep you. Perhaps I will see you tomorrow. It was very strange that we should meet."

"Yes," I said. "Have them look at the truck tomorrow. Anything we can do."

"Good night," he said. "Good trip."

"Good night," I said. We started off and I saw him walking toward the fire waving an arm at the natives. I had not asked him why he had twenty up-country natives with him, nor where he was going. Looking back, I had asked him nothing. I do not like to ask questions, and where I was brought up it was not polite. But here we had not seen a white man for two weeks, not since we had left Babati to go south, and then to run into one on this road where you met only an occasional Indian trader and the steady migration of the natives out of the famine country, to have him look like a caricature of Benchley in Tyrolean costume, to have him know your name, to call you a poet, to have read the *Querschnitt,* to be an admirer of Joachim Ringelnatz and to want to talk about Rilke, was too fantastic to deal with. So, just then, to crown this fantasy, the lights of the car showed three tall, conical, mounds of something smoking in the road ahead. I motioned to Kamau to stop, and putting on the brakes we skidded just short of them. They were from two to three feet high and when I touched one it was quite warm.

"*Tembo,*" M'Cola said.

It was dung from elephants that had just crossed the road, and in the cold of the evening you could see it steaming. In a little while we were in camp.

Next morning I was up and gone to another salt-lick before daylight. There was a kudu bull on the lick when we approached through the trees and he gave a loud bark, like a dog's but higher in pitch and sharply throaty, and was gone, making no noise at first, then crashing in the brush when he was well away; and we never saw him. This lick had an impossible approach. Trees grew around its open area so that it was as though the game were in the blind and you had to come to them across the open. The only way to make it would have been for one man to go alone and crawl and then it would be impossible to get any sort of a close shot through the interlacing trees until you were within twenty yards. Of course once you were inside the protecting trees, and in the blind, you were wonderfully placed, for anything that came to the salt had to come out in the open twenty-five yards from any cover. But though we stayed until eleven o'clock nothing came. We smoothed the dust of the lick carefully with our feet so that any new tracks would show when we came back again and walked the two miles to the road. Being hunted, the game had learned to come only at night and leave before daylight. One bull had stayed and our spooking him that morning would make it even more difficult now.

This was the tenth day we had been hunting greater kudu and I had not seen a mature bull yet. We had only three days more because the rains were moving north each day from Rhodesia and unless we were prepared to stay where we were through the rains we must be out as far as Handeni before they came. We had set the seventeenth of February as the last safe date to leave. Every morning now it took the heavy, wooled sky an hour or so longer to clear and you could feel the rains coming, as they moved steadily north, as surely as though you watched them on a chart.

Now it is pleasant to hunt something that you want very much over a long period of time, being outwitted, out-manœuvred, and failing at the end of each day, but having the hunt and knowing every time you are out that, sooner or later, your luck will change and that you will get the chance that you are seeking. But it is not pleasant to have a time limit by which you must get your kudu or perhaps never get it, nor even see one.

It is not the way hunting should be. It is too much like those boys who used to be sent to Paris with two years in which to make good as writers or painters after which, if they had not made good, they could go home and into their fathers' business. The way to hunt is for as long as you live against as long as there is such and such an animal; just as the way to paint is as long is there is you and colors and canvas, and to write as long as you can live and there is pencil and paper or ink or any machine to do it with, or anything you care to write about, and you feel a fool, and you are a fool, to do it any other way. But here we were, now, caught by time, by the season, and by the running out of our money, so that what should have been as much fun to do each day whether you killed or not was being forced into that most exciting perversion of life; the necessity of accomplishing something in less time than should truly be allowed for its doing. So, coming in at noon, up since two hours before daylight, with only three days left, I was starting to be nervous about it, and there, at the table under the dining tent fly, talking away, was Kandisky of the Tyroler pants. I had forgotten all about him.

"Hello. Hello," he said. "No success? Nothing doing? Where is the kudu?"

"He coughed once and went away," I said. "Heilo, girl."

She smiled. She was worried too. The two of them

had been listening since daylight for a shot. Listening all the time, even when our guest had arrived; listening while writing letters, listening while reading, listening when Kandisky came back and talked.

"You did not shoot him?"

"No. Nor see him." I saw that Pop was worried too, and a little nervous. There had evidently been considerable talking going on.

"Have a beer, Colonel," he said to me.

"We spooked one," I reported. "No chance of a shot. There were plenty of tracks. Nothing more came. The wind was blowing around. Ask the boys about it."

"As I was telling Colonel Phillips," Kandisky began, shifting his leather-breeched behind and crossing one heavy-calved, well-haired, bare leg over the other, "you must not stay here too long. You must realize the rains are coming. There is one stretch of twelve miles beyond here you can never get through if it rains. It is impossible."

"So he's been telling me," Pop said. "I'm a Mister, by the way. We use these military titles as nicknames. No offense if you're a Colonel yourself." Then to me, "Damn these salt-licks. If you'd leave them alone you'd get one."

"They ball it all up," I agreed. "You're so sure of a shot sooner or later on the lick."

"Hunt the hills too."

"I'll hunt them, Pop."

13

"What is killing a kudu, anyway?" Kandisky asked. "You should not take it so seriously. It is nothing. In a year you kill twenty."

"Best not say anything about that to the game department, though," Pop said.

"You misunderstand," Kandisky said. "I mean in a year a man could. Of course no man would wish to."

"Absolutely," Pop said. "If he lived in kudu country, he could. They're the commonest big antelope in this bush country. It's just that when you want to see them you don't."

"I kill nothing, you understand," Kandisky told us. "Why are you not more interested in the natives?"

"We are," my wife assured him.

"They are really interesting. Listen—" Kandisky said, and he spoke on to her.

"The hell of it is," I said to Pop, "when I'm in the hills I'm sure the bastards are down there on the salt. The cows are in the hills but I don't believe the bulls are with them now. Then you get there in the evening and there are the tracks. They *have* been on the lousy salt. I think they come any time."

"Probably they do."

"I'm sure we get different bulls there. They probably only come to the salt every couple of days. Some are certainly spooked because Karl shot that one. If he'd only killed it clean instead of following it through the whole damn countryside. Christ, if he'd only kill any damn thing clean. Other new ones will come in. All we have to do is to wait them out, though. Of course they can't all know about it. But he's spooked this country to hell."

"He gets so very excited," Pop said. "But he's a good lad. He made a beautiful shot on that leopard, you know. You don't want them killed any cleaner than that. Let it quiet down again."

"Sure. I don't mean anything when I curse him."

"What about staying in the blind all day?"

"The damned wind started to go round in a circle. It blew our scent every bloody direction. No bloody use to sit there broadcasting it. If the damn wind would hold. Abdullah took an ash can today."

"I saw him starting off with it."

"There wasn't a bit of wind when we stalked the salt and there was just light to shoot. He tried the wind with the ashes all the way. I went alone with Abdullah and left the others behind and we went quietly. I had on these crepe-soled boots and it's soft cotton dirt. The bastard spooked at fifty yards.

"Did you ever see their ears?"

"Did I ever see their ears? If I can see the bastard's ears, the skinner can work on him."

"They're bastards," Pop said. "I hate this salt-lick business. They're not as smart as we think. The trouble is you're working on them where they are smart. They've been shot at there ever since there's been salt."

15

"That's what makes it fun," I said. "I'd be glad to do it for a month. I like to hunt sitting on my tail. No sweat. No nothing. Sit there and catch flies and feed them to the ant lions in the dust. I like it. But what about the time?"

"That's it. The bloody time."

"So," Kandisky was saying to my wife. "That is what you should see. The big ngomas. The big native dance festivals. The real ones."

"Listen," I said to Pop. "The other lick, the one I was at last night, is fool-proof except for being near that *bloody* road."

"The trackers say it is really the property of the lesser kudu. It's a long way too. It's eighty miles there and back."

"I know. But there were four *big* bull tracks. It's certain. If it wasn't for that truck last night. What about staying there tonight? Then I'd get the night and the early morning and give this lick a rest. There's a big rhino there too. Big track, anyway."

"Good," Pop said. "Shoot the damn rhino too." He hated to have anything killed except what we were after, no killing on the side, no ornamental killing, no killing to kill, only when you wanted it more than you wanted not to kill it, only when getting it was necessary to his being first in his trade, and I saw he was offering up the rhino to please me.

"I won't kill him unless he's good," I promised.

16

"Shoot the bastard," Pop said, making a gift of him.

"Ah, Pop," I said.

"Shoot him," said Pop. "You'll enjoy it, being by yourself. You can sell the horn if you don't want it. You've still one on your license."

"So," said Kandisky. "You have arrested a plan of campaign? You have decided on how to outwit the poor animals?"

"Yes," I said. "How is the truck?"

"That lorry is finished," the Austrian said. "In a way I am glad. It was too much of a symbol. It was all that remained of my shamba. Now everything is gone and it is much simpler."

"What is a shamba?" asked P. O. M., my wife. "I've been hearing about them for months. I'm afraid to ask about those words every one uses."

"A plantation," he said. "It is all gone except that lorry. With the lorry I carry laborers to the shamba of an Indian. It is a very rich Indian who raises sisal. I am a manager for this Indian. An Indian can make a profit from a sisal shamba."

"From anything," Pop said.

"Yes. Where we fail, where we would starve, he makes money. This Indian is very intelligent, however. He values me. I represent European organization. I come now from organizing recruitment of the natives. This takes time. It is impressive. I have been away from my family for three months. The organization is

17

organized. You do it in a week as easily, but it is not so impressive."

"And your wife?" asked mine.

"She waits at my house, the house of the manager, with my daughter."

"Does she love you very much?" my wife asked.

"She must, or she would be gone long ago."

"How old is the daughter?"

"She is thirteen now."

"It must be very nice to have a daughter."

"You cannot know how nice it is. It is like a second wife. My wife knows now all I think, all I say, all I believe, all I can do, all that I cannot do and cannot be. I know also about my wife—completely. But now there is always someone you do not know, who does not know you, who loves you in ignorance and is strange to you both. Some one very attractive that is yours and not yours and that makes the conversation more—how shall I say? Yes, it is like—what do you call—having here with you—with the two of you—yes there— It is the Heinz Tomato Ketchup on the daily food."

"That's very good," I said.

"We have books," he said. "I cannot buy new books now but we can always talk. Ideas and conversation are very interesting. We discuss all things. Everything. We have a very interesting mental life. Formerly, with the shamba, we had the *Querschnitt*. That gave you a feeling of belonging, of being made a part of, to a very

18

brilliant group of people. The people one would see if one saw whom one wished to see. You know all of those people? You must know them."

"Some of them," I said. "Some in Paris. Some in Berlin."

I did not wish to destroy anything this man had, and so I did not go into those brilliant people in detail.

"They're marvellous," I said, lying.

"I envy you to know them," he said. "And tell me, who is the greatest writer in America?"

"My husband," said my wife.

"No. I do not mean for you to speak from family pride. I mean who really? Certainly not Upton Sinclair. Certainly not Sinclair Lewis. Who is your Thomas Mann? Who is your Valery?"

"We do not have great writers," I said. "Something happens to our good writers at a certain age. I can explain but it is quite long and may bore you."

"Please explain," he said. "This is what I enjoy. This is the best part of life. The life of the mind. This is not killing kudu."

"You haven't heard it yet," I said.

"Ah, but I can see it coming. You must take more beer to loosen your tongue."

"It's loose," I told him. "It's always too bloody loose. But *you* don't drink anything."

"No, I never drink. It is not good for the mind. It is unnecessary. But tell me. Please tell me."

"Well," I said, "we have had, in America, skillful writers. Poe is a skillful writer. It is skillful, marvellously constructed, and it is dead. We have had writers of rhetoric who had the good fortune to find a little, in a chronicle of another man and from voyaging, of how things, actual things, can be, whales for instance, and this knowledge is wrapped in the rhetoric like plums in a pudding. Occasionally it is there, alone, unwrapped in pudding, and it is good. This is Melville. But the people who praise it, praise it for the rhetoric which is not important. They put a mystery in which is not there."

"Yes," he said. "I see. But it is the mind working, its ability to work, which makes the rhetoric. Rhetoric is the blue sparks from the dynamo."

"Sometimes. And sometimes it is only blue sparks and what is the dynamo driving?"

"So. Go on."

"I've forgotten."

"No. Go on. Do not pretend to be stupid."

"Did you ever get up before daylight——"

"Every morning," he said. "Go on."

"All right. There were others who wrote like exiled English colonials from an England of which they were never a part to a newer England that they were making. Very good men with the small, dried, and excellent wisdom of Unitarians; men of letters; Quakers with a sense of humor."

"Who were these?"

"Emerson, Hawthorne, Whittier, and Company. All our early classics who did not know that a new classic does not bear any resemblance to the classics that have preceded it. It can steal from anything that it is better than, anything that is not a classic, all classics do that. Some writers are only born to help another writer to write one sentence. But it cannot derive from or resemble a previous classic. Also all these men were gentlemen, or wished to be. They were all very respectable. They did not use the words that people always have used in speech, the words that survive in language. Nor would you gather that they had bodies. They had minds, yes. Nice, dry, clean minds. This is all very dull, I would not state it except that you ask for it."

"Go on."

"There is one at that time that is supposed to be really good, Thoreau. I cannot tell you about it because I have not yet been able to read it. But that means nothing because I cannot read other naturalists unless they are being extremely accurate and not literary. Naturalists should all work alone and some one else should correlate their findings for them. Writers should work alone. They should see each other only after their work is done, and not too often then. Otherwise they become like writers in New York. All angleworms in a bottle, trying to derive knowledge and nourishment from their own contact and from the bottle. Sometimes the bottle is shaped art, sometimes economics, sometimes economicreligion. But once they are in the bottle they stay there. They are lonesome outside of the bottle. They do not want to be lonesome. They are afraid to be alone in their beliefs and no woman would love any of them enough so that they could kill their lonesomeness in that woman, or pool it with hers, or make something with her that makes the rest unimportant."

"But what about Thoreau?"

"You'll have to read him. Maybe I'll be able to later. I can do nearly everything later."

"Better have some more beer, Papa."

"All right."

"What about the good writers?"

"The good writers are Henry James, Stephen Crane, and Mark Twain. That's not the order they're good in. There is no order for good writers."

"Mark Twain is a humorist. The others I do not know."

"All modern American literature comes from one book by Mark Twain called *Huckleberry Finn*. If you read it you must stop where the Nigger Jim is stolen from the boys. That is the real end. The rest is just cheating. But it's the best book we've had. All American writing comes from that. There was nothing before. There has been nothing as good since."

"What about the others?"

"Crane wrote two fine stories. *The Open Boat* and *The Blue Hotel*. The last one is the best."

"And what happened to him?"

"He died. That's simple. He was dying from the start."

"But the other two?"

"They both lived to be old men but they did not get any wiser as they got older. I don't know what they really wanted. You see we make our writers into something very strange."

"I do not understand."

"We destroy them in many ways. First, economically. They make money. It is only by hazard that a writer makes money although good books always make money eventually. Then our writers when they have made some money increase their standard of living and they are caught. They have to write to keep up their establishments, their wives, and so on, and they write slop. It is slop not on purpose but because it is hurried. Because they write when there is nothing to say or no water in the well. Because they are ambitious. Then, once they have betrayed themselves, they justify it and you get more slop. Or else they read the critics. If they believe the critics when they say they are great then they must believe them when they say they are rotten and they lose confidence. At present we have two good writers who cannot write because they have lost confidence through reading critics. If they wrote, sometimes it would be good and sometimes not so good and sometimes it would be quite bad, but the good would get out. But they have read the critics and they must write masterpieces. The masterpieces the critics said they wrote. They weren't masterpieces, of course. They were just quite good books. So now they cannot write at all. The critics have made them impotent.

"Who are these writers?"

"Their names would mean nothing to you and by now they may have written, become frightened, and be impotent again."

"But what is it that happens to American writers? Be definite."

"I was not here in the old days so I cannot tell you about them, but now there are various things. At a certain age the men writers change into Old Mother Hubbard. The women writers become Joan of Arc without the fighting. They become leaders. It doesn't matter who they lead. If they do not have followers they invent them. It is useless for those selected as followers to protest. They are accused of disloyalty. Oh, hell. There are too many things happen to them. That is one thing. The others try to save their souls with what they write. That is an easy way out. Others are ruined by the first money, the first praise, the first attack, the first time they find they cannot write, or the first time they cannot do anything else, or else they get frightened and join organizations that do their thinking for them. Or they do not know what they want. Henry James wanted to make money. He never did, of course."

"And you?"

"I am interested in other things. I have a good life but I must write because if I do not write a certain amount I do not enjoy the rest of my life."

"And what do you want?"

"To write as well as I can and learn as I go along. At the same time I have my life which I enjoy and which is a damned good life."

"Hunting kudu?"

"Yes. Hunting kudu and many other things."

"What other things?"

"Plenty of other things."

"And you know what you want?"

"Yes."

"You really like to do this, what you do now, this silliness of kudu?"

"Just as much as I like to be in the Prado."

"One is not better than the other?"

"One is as necessary as the other. There are other things, too."

"Naturally. There must be. But this sort of thing means something to you, really?"

"Truly."

"And you know what you want?"

"Absolutely, and I get it all the time."

"But it takes money."

"I could always make money and besides I have been very lucky."

"Then you are happy?"

"Except when I think of other people."

"Then you think of other people?"

"Oh, yes."

"But you do nothing for them?"

"No."

"Nothing?"

"Maybe a little."

"Do you think your writing is worth doing—as an end in itself?"

"Oh, yes."

"You are sure?"

"Very sure."

"That must be very pleasant."

"It is," I said. "It is the one altogether pleasant thing about it."

"This is getting awfully serious," my wife said.

"It's a damned serious subject."

"You see, he is really serious about something," Kandisky said. "I knew he must be serious on something besides kudu."

"The reason every one now tries to avoid it, to deny that it is important, to make it seem vain to try to do it, is because it is so difficult. Too many factors must combine to make it possible."

"What is this now?"

"The kind of writing that can be done. How far prose can be carried if any one is serious enough and has luck.

There is a fourth and fifth dimension that can be gotten."

"You believe it?"

"I know it."

"And if a writer can get this?"

"Then nothing else matters. It is more important than anything he can do. The chances are, of course, that he will fail. But there is a chance that he succeeds."

"But that is poetry you are talking about."

"No. It is much more difficult than poetry. It is a prose that has never been written. But it can be written, without tricks and without cheating. With nothing that will go bad afterwards."

"And why has it not been written?"

"Because there are too many factors. First, there must be talent, much talent. Talent such as Kipling had. Then there must be discipline. The discipline of Flaubert. Then there must be the conception of what it can be and an absolute conscience as unchanging as the standard meter in Paris, to prevent faking. Then the writer must be intelligent and disinterested and above all he must survive. Try to get all these in one person and have him come through all the influences that press on a writer. The hardest thing, because time is so short, is for him to survive and get his work done. But I would like us to have such a writer and to read what he would write. What do you say? Should we talk about something else?"

"It is interesting what you say. Naturally I do not agree with everything."

"Naturally."

"What about a gimlet?" Pop asked. "Don't you think a gimlet might help?"

"Tell me first what are the things, the actual, concrete things that harm a writer?"

I was tired of the conversation which was becoming an interview. So I would make it an interview and finish it. The necessity to put a thousand intangibles into a sentence, now, before lunch, was too bloody.

"Politics, women, drink, money, ambition. And the lack of politics, women, drink, money and ambition," I said profoundly.

"He's getting much too easy now," Pop said.

"But drink. I do not understand about that. That has always seemed silly to me. I understand it as a weakness."

"It is a way of ending a day. It has great benefits. Don't you ever want to change your ideas?"

"Let's have one," Pop said. "M'Wendi!"

Pop never drank before lunch except as a mistake and I knew he was trying to help me out.

"Let's all have a gimlet," I said.

"I never drink," Kandisky said. "I will go to the lorry and fetch some fresh butter for lunch. It is fresh from Kandoa, un-salted. Very good. Tonight we will have a special dish of Viennese dessert. My cook has learned to make it very well."

He went off and my wife said: "You were getting awfully profound. What was that about all these women?"

"What women?"

"When you were talking about women."

"The hell with them," I said. "Those are the ones you get involved with when you're drunk."

"So that's what you do."

"No."

"I don't get involved with people when I'm drunk."

"Come, come," said Pop. "We're none of us ever drunk. My God, that man can talk."

"He didn't have a chance to talk after B'wana M'Kumba started."

"I did have verbal dysentery," I said.

"What about his lorry? Can we tow it in without ruining ours?"

"I think so," Pop said. "When ours comes back from Handeni."

At lunch under the green fly of the dining tent, in the shade of a big tree, the wind blowing, the fresh butter much admired, Grant's gazelle chops, mashed potatoes, green corn, and then mixed fruit for dessert, Kandisky told us why the East Indians were taking the country over.

"You see, during the war they sent the Indian troops to fight here. To keep them out of India because they feared another mutiny. They promised the Aga Khan that because they fought in Africa, Indians could come freely to settle and for business afterwards. They cannot break that promise and now the Indians have taken the country over from the Europeans. They live on nothing and they send all the money back to India. When they have made enough to go home they leave, bringing out their poor relations to take over from them and continue to exploit the country."

Pop said nothing. He would not argue with a guest at table.

"It is the Aga Khan," Kandisky said. "You aré an American. You know nothing of these combinations."

"Were you with Von Lettöw?" Pop asked him.

"From the start," Kandisky said. "Until the end."

"He was a great fighter," Pop said. "I have great admiration for him."

"You fought?" Kandisky asked.

"Yes."

"I do not care for Lettöw," Kandisky said. "He fought, yes. No one ever better. When we wanted quinine he would order it captured. All supplies the same. But afterwards he cared nothing for his men. After the war I am in Germany. I go to see about indemnification for my property. 'You are an Austrian,' they say. 'You must go through Austrian channels.' So I go to Austria.

'But why did you fight?' they ask me. 'You cannot hold us responsible. Suppose you go to fight in China. That is your own affair. We cannot do anything for you.'

" 'But I went as a patriot,' I say, very foolishly. 'I fight where I can because I am an Austrian and I know my duty.' 'Yes,' they say. 'That is very beautiful. But you cannot hold us responsible for your noble sentiments.' So they passed me from one to the other and nothing. Still I love the country very much. I have lost everything here but I have more than anyone has in Europe. To me it is always interesting. The natives and the language. I have many books of notes on them. Then too, in reality, I am a king here. It is very pleasant. Waking in the morning I extend one foot and the boy places the sock on it. When I am ready I extend the other foot and he adjusts the other sock. I step from under the mosquito bar into my drawers which are held for me. Don't you think that is very marvellous?"

"It's marvellous."

"When you come back another time we must take a safari to study the natives. And shoot nothing, or only to eat. Look, I will show you a dance and sing a song."

Crouched, elbows lifting and falling, knees humping, he shuffled around the table, singing. Undoubtedly it was very fine.

"That is only one of a thousand," he said. "Now I must go for a time. You will be sleeping."

"There's no hurry. Stay around."

"No. Surely you will be sleeping. I also. I will take the butter to keep it cool."

"We'll see you at supper," Pop said.

"Now you must sleep. Good-bye."

After he was gone, Pop said: "I wouldn't believe all that about the Aga Khan, you know."

"It sounded pretty good."

"Of course he feels badly," Pop said. "Who wouldn't. Von Lettöw was a hell of a man."

"He's very intelligent," my wife said. "He talks wonderfully about the natives. But he's bitter about American women."

"So am I," said Pop. "He's a good man. You better get some shut-eye. You'll •need to start about three-thirty."

"Have them call me."

Molo raised the back of the tent, propping it with sticks, so the wind blew through and I went to sleep reading, the wind coming in cool and fresh under the heated canvas.

When I woke it was time to go. There were rain clouds in the sky and it was very hot. They had packed some tinned fruit, a five-pound piece of roast meat, bread, tea, a tea pot, and some tinned milk in a whiskey box with four bottles of beer. There was a canvas water bag and a ground cloth to use as a tent. M'Cola was taking the big gun out to the car.

"There's no hurry about getting back," Pop said. "We'll look for you when we see you."

"All right."

"We'll send the truck to haul that sportsman into Handeni. He's sending his men ahead walking."

"You're sure the truck can stand it? Don't do it because he's a friend of mine."

"Have to get him out. The truck will be in tonight."

"The Memsahib's still asleep," I said. "Maybe she can get out for a walk and shoot some guineas."

"I'm here," she said. "Don't worry about us. *Oh,* I hope you get them."

"Don't send out to look for us along the road until day after tomorrow," I said. "If there's a good chance we'll stay."

"Good luck."

"Good luck, sweet. Good-bye, Mr. J. P."

CHAPTER

WE were out from under the shade of camp and along the sandy river of a road, driving into the western sun, the bush thick to the edge of the sand, solid as a thicket, the little hills rising above it, and all along the road we passed groups of people making their way to the westward. Some were naked except for a greasy cloth knotted over one shoulder, and carried bows and sealed quivers of arrows. Others carried spears. The wealthy carried umbrellas and wore draped white cloth and their women walked behind them, with their pots and pans. Bundles and loads of skins were scattered along ahead on the heads of other natives. All were travelling away

TWO

from the famine. And in the heat, my feet out over
the side of the car to keep them away from the heat
of the engine, hat low over the eyes against the sun,
watching the road, the people, and all clearings in the
bush for game, we drove to the westward.

Once we saw three lesser kudu cows in an open place
of broken bush. Gray, big bellied, long necked, small
headed, and with big ears, they moved quickly into the
woods and were gone. We left the car and tracked them
but there was no bull track.

A little beyond there a flock of guineas quick-legged
across the road running steady-headed with the motion

of trotters. As I jumped from the car and sprinted after them they rocketed up, their legs tucked close beneath them, heavy-bodied, short wings drumming, cackling, to go over the trees ahead. I dropped two that thumped hard when they fell and as they lay, wings beating, Abdullah cut their heads off so they would be legal eating. He put them in the car where M'Cola sat laughing; his old man's healthy laugh, his making-fun-of-me laugh, his bird-shooting laugh that dated from a streak of raging misses one time that had delighted him. Now when I killed, it was a joke as when we shot a hyena; the funniest joke of all. He laughed always to see the birds tumble and when I missed he roared and shook his head again and again.

"Ask him what the hell he's laughing about?" I asked Pop once.

"At B'wana," M'Cola said, and shook his head, "at the little birds."

"He thinks you're funny," Pop said.

"Goddam it. I am funny. But the hell with him."

"He thinks you're very funny," Pop said. "Now the Memsahib and I would never laugh."

"Shoot them yourself."

"No, you're the bird shot. The self-confessed bird shot," she said.

So bird shooting became this marvellous joke. If I killed, the joke was on the birds and M'Cola would shake his head and laugh and make his hands go round and round to show how the bird turned over in the air. And if I missed, I was the clown of the piece and he would look at me and shake with laughing. Only the hyenas were funnier.

Highly humorous was the hyena obscenely loping, full belly dragging, at daylight on the plain, who, shot from the stern, skittered on into speed to tumble end over end. Mirth provoking was the hyena that stopped out of range by an alkali lake to look back and, hit in the chest, went over on his back, his four feet and his full belly in the air. Nothing could be more jolly than the hyena coming suddenly wedge-headed and stinking out of high grass by a *donga,* hit at ten yards, who raced his tail in three narrowing, scampering circles until he died.

It was funny to M'Cola to see a hyena shot at close range. There was that comic slap of the bullet and the hyena's agitated surprise to find death inside of him. It was funnier to see a hyena shot at a great distance, in the heat shimmer of the plain, to see him go over backwards, to see him start that frantic circle, to see that electric speed that meant that he was racing the little nickelled death inside him. But the great joke of all, the thing M'Cola waved his hands across his face about, and turned away and shook his head and laughed, ashamed even of the hyena; the pinnacle of hyenic humor, was the hyena, the classic hyena, that hit too far back while running, would circle madly, snapping and tearing at himself until he pulled his own intestines out, and then stood there, jerking them out and eating them with relish.

"Fisi," M'Cola would say and shake his head in delighted sorrow at there being such an awful beast. Fisi, the hyena, hermaphroditic, self-eating devourer of the dead, trailer of calving cows, ham-stringer, potential biter-off of your face at night while you slept, sad yowler, camp-follower, stinking, foul, with jaws that crack the bones the lion leaves, belly dragging, loping away on the brown plain, looking back, mongrel dog-smart in the face; whack from the little Mannlicher and then the horrid circle starting. *"Fisi,"* M'Cola laughed, ashamed of him, shaking his bald black head. *"Fisi.* Eats himself. *Fisi."*

The hyena was a dirty joke but bird shooting was a clean joke. My whiskey was a clean joke. There were many variations of that joke. Some we come to later. The Mohammedans and all religions were a joke. A joke on all the people who had them. Charo, the other gun bearer, was short, very serious and highly religious. All Ramadan he never swallowed his saliva until sunset and when the sun was almost down I'd see him watching nervously. He had a bottle with him of some sort of tea and he would finger it and watch the sun and I would see M'Cola watching him and pretending not to see. This was not outrightly funny to him. This was something that he could not laugh about openly but that he felt superior to and wondered at the silliness of it. The Mohammedan religion was very fashionable and

38

all the higher social grades among the boys were Mohammedans. It was something that gave caste, something to believe in, something fashionable and god-giving
to suffer a little for each year, something that made you
superior to other people, something that gave you more
complicated habits of eating, something that I understood and M'Cola did not understand, nor care about,
and he watched Charo watch for the sun to set with that
blank look on his face that it put on about all things
that he was not a part of. Charo was deadly thirsty
and truly devout and the sun set very slowly. I looked
at it, red over the trees, nudged him and he grinned.
M'Cola offered me the water bottle solemnly. I shook
my head and Charo grinned again. M'Cola looked blank.
Then the sun was down and Charo had the bottle tilted
up, his Adam's apple rising and falling greedily and
M'Cola looking at him and then looking away.

In the early days, before we became good friends, he
did not trust me at all. When anything came up he went
into this blankness. I liked Charo much better then.
We understood each other on the question of religion
and Charo admired my shooting and always shook hands
and smiled when we had killed anything particularly
good. This was flattering and pleasing. M'Cola looked
on all this early shooting as a series of lucky accidents.
We were supposed to shoot. We had not yet shot anything that amounted to anything and he was not really
my gun bearer. He was Mr. Jackson Phillip's gun bearer

and he had been loaned to me. I meant nothing to him. He did not like me nor dislike me. He was politely contemptuous of Karl. Who he liked was Mama.

The evening we killed the first lion it was dark when we came in sight of camp. The killing of the lion had been confused and unsatisfactory. It was agreed beforehand that P. O. M. should have the first shot but since it was the first lion any of us had ever shot at, and it was very late in the day, really too late to take the lion on, once he was hit we were to make a dogfight of it and any one was free to get him. This was a good plan as it was nearly sundown and if the lion got into cover, wounded, it would be too dark to do anything about it without a mess. I remember seeing the lion looking yellow and heavy-headed and enormous against a scrubby-looking tree in a patch of orchard bush and P. O. M. kneeling to shoot and wanting to tell her to sit down and make sure of him. Then there was the short-barrelled explosion of the Mannlicher and the lion was going to the left on a run, a strange, heavy-shouldered, foot-swinging, cat run. I hit him with the Springfield and he went down and spun over and I shot again, too quickly, and threw a cloud of dirt over him. But there he was, stretched out, on his belly, and, with the sun just over the top of the trees, and the grass very green, we walked up on him like a posse, or a gang of Black and Tans, guns ready and cocked, not knowing whether he was stunned or dead. When we were close M'Cola threw a stone at him. It hit him in the flank and from the way it hit you could tell he was a dead animal. I was sure P. O. M. had hit him but there was only one bullet hole, well back, just below the spine and ranging forward to come to the surface under the skin of the chest. You could feel the bullet under the skin and M'Cola made a slit and cut it out. It was a 220-grain solid bullet from the Springfield and it had raked him, going through lungs and heart.

I was so surprised by the way he had rolled over dead from the shot after we had been prepared for a charge, for heroics, and for drama, that I felt more let down than pleased. It was our first lion and we were very ignorant and this was not what we had paid to see. Charo and M'Cola both shook P. O. M.'s hand and then Charo came over and shook hands with me.

"Good shot, B'wana," he said in Swahili. *"Piga m'uzuri."*

"Did you shoot, Karl?" I asked.

"No. I was just going to when you shot."

"You didn't shoot him, Pop?"

"No. You'd have heard it." He opened the breech and took out the two big .450 No. 2's.

"I'm sure I missed him," P. O. M. said.

"I was sure you hit him. I still think you hit him," I said.

"Mama hit," M'Cola said.

"Where?" Charo asked.

"Hit," said M'Cola. "Hit."

"You rolled him over," Pop said to me. "God, he went over like a rabbit."

"I couldn't believe it."

"Mama *piga*," M'Cola said. *"Piga Simba."*

As we saw the camp fire in the dark ahead of us, coming in that night, M'Cola suddenly commenced to shout a stream of high-pitched, rapid, singing words in Wakamba ending in the word *"Simba."* Some one at the camp shouted back one word.

"Mama!" M'Cola shouted. Then another long stream. Then "Mama! Mama!"

Through the dark came all the porters, the cook, the skinner, the boys, and the headman.

"Mama!" M'Cola shouted. "Mama *piga Simba."*

The boys came dancing, crowding, and beating time and chanting something from down in their chests that started like a cough and sounded like *"Hey la Mama! Hay la Mama! Hey la Mama!"*

The rolling-eyed skinner picked P. O. M. up, the big cook and the boys held her, and the others pressing forward to lift, and if not to lift to touch and hold, they danced and sang through the dark, around the fire and to our tent.

"Hey la Mama! huh! huh! huh! Hay la Mama! huh! huh! huh!" they sang the lion dance with that deep, lion asthmatic cough in it. Then at the tent they put her down and every one, very shyly, shook hands, the boys

saying *"m'uzuri, Memsahib,"* and M'Cola and the porters all saying *"m'uzuri,* Mama" with much feeling in the accenting of the word "Mama."

Afterwards in the chairs in front of the fire, sitting with the drinks, Pop said, "You shot it. M'Cola would kill any one who said you didn't."

"You know, I feel as though I did shoot it," P. O. M. said. "I don't believe I'd be able to stand it if I really had shot it. I'd be too proud. Isn't triumph marvellous?"

"Good old Mama," Karl said.

"I believe you did shoot him," I said.

"Oh, let's not go into that," P. O. M. said. "I feel so wonderful about just being supposed to have killed him. You know people never used to carry me on their shoulders much at home."

"No one knows how to behave in America," Pop said. "Most uncivilized."

"We'll carry you in Key West," Karl said. "Poor old Mama."

"Let's not talk about it," P. O. M. said. "I like it too much. Shouldn't I maybe distribute largess?"

"They didn't do it for that," Pop said. "But it is all right to give something to celebrate."

"Oh, I want to give them all a great deal of money," P. O. M. said. "Isn't triumph simply marvellous?"

"Good old Mama," I said. "You killed him."

"No I didn't. Don't lie to me. Just let me enjoy my triumph."

Anyway M'Cola did not trust me for a long time. Until P. O. M.'s license ran out, she was his favorite and we were simply a lot of people who interfered and kept Mama from shooting things. Once her license was out and she was no longer shooting, she dropped back into non-combatant status with him and as we began to hunt kudu and Pop stayed in camp and sent us out alone with the trackers, Karl with Charo and M'Cola and I together, M'Cola dropped Pop visibly in his estimation. It was only temporary of course. He was Pop's man and I believe his working estimations were only from day to day and required an unbroken series of events to have any meaning. But something had happened between us.

GREEN HILLS OF AFRICA

PART II

Pursuit Remembered

CHAPTER

I T dated back to the time of Droopy, after I had come
back from being ill in Nairobi and we had gone on a
foot safari to hunt rhino in the forest. Droopy was a
real savage with lids to his eyes that nearly covered them,
handsome, with a great deal of style, a fine hunter and
a beautiful tracker. He was about thirty-five, I should
think, and wore only a piece of cloth, knotted over one
shoulder, and a fez that some hunter had given him.
He always carried a spear. M'Cola wore an old U. S.
Army khaki tunic, complete with buttons, that had orig-
inally been brought out for Droopy who had been **away**

46

THREE

somewhere and had missed getting it. Twice Pop had
brought it out for Droopy and finally M'Cola had said,
"Give it to me."

Pop had let him have it and M'Cola had worn it ever
since. It, a pair of shorts, his fuzzy wool curler's cap,
and a knitted army sweater he wore when washing the
tunic, were the only garments I ever saw on the old man
until he took my bird-shooting coat. For shoes he used
sandals cut from old motor-car tires. He had slim, handsome legs with well-turned ankles on the style of Babe
Ruth's and I remember how surprised I was the first

47

time I saw him with the tunic off and noticed how old his upper body was. It had that aged look you see in photographs of Jeffries and Sharkey posing thirty years after, the ugly, old-man biceps and the fallen pectoral muscles.

"How old is M'Cola?" I asked Pop.

"He must be over fifty," Pop said. "He's got a grown-up family in the native reserve."

"How are his kids?"

"No good, worthless. He can't handle them. We tried one as a porter. But he was no good."

M'Cola was not jealous of Droopy. He simply knew that Droop was a better man than he was. More of a hunter, a faster and a cleaner tracker, and a great stylist in everything he did. He admired Droopy in the same way we did and being out with him, it made him realize that he was wearing Droopy's tunic and that he had been a porter before he became a gun bearer and suddenly he ceased being an old timer and we were hunting together; he and I hunting together and Droopy in command of the show.

That had been a fine hunt. The afternoon of the day we came into the country we walked about four miles from camp along a deep rhino trail that graded through the grassy hills with their abandoned orchard-looking trees, as smoothly and evenly as though an engineer had planned it. The trail was a foot deep in the ground and smoothly worn and we left it where it slanted down through a divide in the hills like a dry irrigation ditch and climbed, sweating, the small, steep hill on the right to sit there with our backs against the hilltop and glass the country. It was a green, pleasant country, with hills below the forest that grew thick on the side of a mountain, and it was cut by the valleys of several watercourses that came down out of the thick timber on the mountain. Fingers of the forest came down onto the heads of some of the slopes and it was there, at the forest edge, that we watched for rhino to come out. If you looked away from the forest and the mountain side you could follow the watercourses and the hilly slope of the land down until the land flattened and the grass was brown and burned and, away, across a long sweep of country, was the brown Rift Valley and the shine of Lake Manyara.

We all lay there on the hillside and watched the country carefully for rhino. Droopy was on the other side of the hilltop, squatted on his heels, looking, and M'Cola sat below us. There was a cool breeze from the east and it blew the grass in waves on the hillsides. There were many large white clouds and the tall trees of the forest on the mountain side grew so closely and were so foliaged that it looked as though you could walk on their tops. Behind this mountain there was a gap and then another mountain and the far mountain was dark blue with forest in the distance.

Until five o'clock we did not see anything. Then, without the glasses, I saw something moving over the shoulder of one of the valleys toward a strip of the timber. In the glasses it was a rhino, showing very clear and minute at the distance, red-colored in the sun, moving with a quick waterbug-like motion across the hill. Then there were three more of them that came out of the forest, dark in the shadow, and two that fought, tinily, in the glasses, pushing head-on, fighting in front of a clump of bushes while we watched them and the light failed. It was too dark to get down the hill, across the valley and up the narrow slope of mountain side to them in time for a shot. So we went back to the camp, down the hill in the dark, edging down on our shoes and then feeling the trail smooth under foot, walking along that deep trail, that wound through the dark hills, until we saw the firelight in the trees.

We were excited that night because we had seen the three rhino and early the next morning while we were eating breakfast before starting out, Droopy came in to report a herd of buffalo he had found feeding at the edge of the forest not two miles from camp. We went there, still tasting coffee and kippers in the early morning heart-pounding of excitement, and the native Droopy had left watching them pointed where they had crossed a deep gulch and gone into an open patch of forest. He said there were two big bulls in a herd of a dozen or more. We followed them in, moving very quietly on the game trails, pushing the vines aside and seeing the tracks and the quantities of fresh dung, but though we went on into the forest where it was too thick to shoot and made a wide circle, we did not see or hear them. Once we heard the tick birds and saw them flying, but that was all. There were numbers of rhino trails there in the woods and many strawy piles of dung, but we saw nothing but the green wood-pigeons and some monkeys, and when we came out we were wet to our waists from the dew and the sun was quite high. The day was very hot, now before the wind had gotten up, and we knew whatever rhino and buffalo had been out would have gone back deep into the forest to rest out of the heat.

The others started back to camp with Pop and M'Cola. There was no meat in camp and I wanted to hunt back in a circle with Droopy to see if we could kill a piece. I was beginning to feel strong again after the dysentery and it was a pleasure to walk in the easy rolling country, simply to walk, and to be able to hunt, not knowing what we might see and free to shoot for the meat we needed. Then, too, I liked Droopy and liked to watch him walk. He strode very loosely and with a slight lift, and I liked to watch him and to feel the grass under my soft-soled shoes and the pleasant weight of the rifle, held just back of the muzzle, the barrel resting on my shoulder, and the sun hot enough to sweat you well as it burned the dew from the grass; with the breeze starting and the country like an abandoned New England orchard to walk through. I knew that I was shooting well again and I wanted to make a shot to impress Droopy.

From the top of one rise we saw two kongoni showing yellow on a hillside about a mile away and I motioned to Droop that we would go after them. We started down and in a ravine jumped a waterbuck bull and two cows. Waterbuck was the one animal we might get that I knew was worthless as meat and I had shot a better head than this one carried. I had the sights on the buck as he tore away, remembered about the worthless meat, and having the head, and did not shoot.

"No shoot kuro?" Droopy asked in Swahili. *"Doumi sana.* A good bull."

I tried to tell him that I had a better one and that it was no good to eat.

He grinned.

"Piga kongoni m'uzuri."

"Piga" was a fine word. It sounded exactly as the command to fire should sound or the announcement of a hit. "M'uzuri," meaning good, well, better, had sounded too much like the name of a state for a long time and walking I used to make up sentences in Swahili with Arkansas and M'uzuri in them, but now it seemed natural, no longer to be italicized, just as all the words came to seem the proper and natural words and there was nothing odd or unseemly in the stretching of the ears, in the tribal scars, or in a man carrying a spear. The tribal marks and the tattooed places seemed natural and handsome adornments and I regretted not having any of my own. My own scars were all informal, some irregular and sprawling, others simply puffy welts. I had one on my forehead that people still commented on, asking if I had bumped my head; but Droop had handsome ones beside his cheekbones and others, symmetrical and decorative, on his chest and belly. I was thinking that I had one good one, a sort of embossed Christmas tree, on the bottom of my right foot that only served to wear out socks, when we jumped two reedbuck. They went off through the trees and then stood at sixty yards, the thin, graceful buck looking back, and I shot him high and a touch behind the shoulder. He gave a jump and went off very fast.

"Piga." Droopy smiled. We had both heard the whunk of the bullet.

"Kufa," I told him. "Dead."

But when we came up to him, lying on his side, his heart was still beating strongly, although to all appearances he was dead. Droopy had no skinning knife and I had only a penknife to stick him with. I felt for the heart behind the foreleg with my fingers and feeling it beating under the hide slipped the knife in but it was short and pushed the heart away. I could feel it, hot and rubbery against my fingers, and feel the knife push it, but I felt around and cut the big artery and the blood came hot against my fingers. Once bled, I started to open him, with the little knife, still showing off to Droopy, and emptying him neatly took out the liver, cut away the gall, and laying the liver on a hummock of grass, put the kidneys beside it.

Droopy asked for the knife. Now he was going to show me something. Skilfully he slit open the stomach and turned it inside, tripe side, out, emptying the grass in it on the ground, shook it, then put the liver and kidneys inside it and with the knife cut a switch from the tree the buck lay under and sewed the stomach together with the withe so that the tripe made a bag to carry the other delicacies in. Then he cut a pole and put the bag on the end of it, running it through the flaps, and put it over his shoulder in the way tramps carried their property in a handkerchief on the end of a stick in Blue Jay corn plaster advertisements when we were children. It was a good trick and I thought how I would show it to John Staib in Wyoming some time and he would smile his deaf man's smile (you had to throw pebbles at him to make him stop when you heard a bull bugle), and I knew what John would say. He would say, "By Godd, Urnust, dot's smardt."

Droop handed me the stick, then took off his single garment, made a sling and got the buck up on his back. I tried to help him and suggested by signs that we cut a pole and sling him, carrying him between us, but he wanted to carry him alone. So we started for camp, me with the tripe bag on the end of a stick over my shoulder, my rifle slung, and Droopy staggering steadily ahead, sweating heavily, under the buck. I tried to get him to hang him in a tree and leave him until we could send out a couple of porters, and to that end we put him in the crotch of a tree. But when Droop saw that I meant to go off and leave him there rather than simply allow him to drain he got him down onto his shoulders again and we went on into camp, the boys, around the cooking fire, all laughing at the tripe bag over my shoulder as we came in.

This was the kind of hunting that I liked. No riding in cars, the country broken up instead of the plains, and I was completely happy. I had been quite ill and had that pleasant feeling of getting stronger each day. I was underweight, had a great appetite for meat, and could eat all I wanted without feeling stuffy. Each day I sweated out whatever we drank sitting at the fire at night, and in the heat of the day, now, I lay in the shade with a breeze in the trees and read with no obligation and no compulsion to write, happy in knowing that at four o'clock we would be starting out to hunt again. I would not even write a letter. The only person I really cared about, except the children, was with me and I had no wish to share this life with any one who was not there, only to live it, being completely happy and quite tired. I knew that I was shooting well and I had that feeling of well being and confidence that is so much more pleasant to have than to hear about.

As it turned out, we started soon after three to be on the hill by four. But it was nearly five before we saw the first rhino come bustling short-leggedly across the ridge of hill in almost the same place we had seen the rhino the night before. We saw where he went into the edge of the forest near where we had seen the two fighting and then took a course that would lead us down the hill, across the grown-over gully at the bottom, and up the steep slope to where there was a thorn tree with yellow blossoms that marked the place where we had seen the rhino go in.

Coming straight up the slope in sight of the thorn tree, the wind blowing across the hill, I tried to walk as slowly as I could and put a handkerchief inside the sweatband of my hat to keep the perspiration out of my glasses. I expected to shoot at any minute and I wanted to slow up enough so my heart would not be pounding. In shooting large animals there is no reason ever to miss if you have a clear shot and can shoot and know where to shoot, unless you are unsteady from a run or a climb or fog your glasses, break them or run out of cloth or paper to wipe them clean. The glasses were the biggest hazard and I used to carry four handkerchiefs and change them from the left to the right pocket when they were wet.

We came up to the yellow blossomed tree very carefully, like people walking up to a covey of quail the dogs have pointed, and the rhino was not in sight. We went all through the edge of the forest and it was full of tracks and fresh rhino sign, but there was no rhino. The sun was setting and it was getting too dark to shoot, but we followed the forest around the side of the mountain, hoping to see a rhino in the open glades. When it was almost too dark to shoot, I saw Droopy stop and crouch. With his head down he motioned us forward. Crawling up, we saw a large rhino and a small one standing chest deep in brush, facing us across a little valley.

"Cow and calf," Pop said softly. "Can't shoot her. Let me look at her horn." He took the glasses from M'Cola.

"Can she see us?" P. O. M. asked.

"No."

"How far are they?"

"Must be nearly five hundred yards."

"My God, she looks big," I whispered.

"She's a big cow," Pop said. "Wonder what became of the bull?" He was pleased and excited by the sight of game. "Too dark to shoot unless we're right on him."

The rhinos had turned and were feeding. They never seemed to move slowly. They either bustled or stood still.

"What makes them so red?" P. O. M. asked.

"Rolling in the mud," Pop answered. "We better get along while there's light."

The sun was down when we came out of the forest and looked down the slope and across to the hill where we had watched from with our glasses. We should have back-tracked and gone down, crossed the gulch, and climbed back up the trail the way we had come but we decided, like fools, to grade straight across the mountain side below the edge of the forest. So in the dark, following this ideal line, we descended into steep ravines that showed only as wooded patches until you were in them, slid down, clung to vines, stumbled and climbed and slid again, down and down, then steeply, impossibly, up, hearing the rustle of night things and the cough of a leopard hunting baboons; me scared of snakes and touching each root and branch with snake fear in the dark.

To go down and up two hands-and-knee-climbing ravines and then out into the moonlight and the long, too-steep shoulder of mountain that you climbed one foot up to the other, one foot after the other, one stride at a time, leaning forward against the grade and the altitude, dead tired and gun weary, single file in the moonlight across the slope, on up and to the top where it was easy, the country spread in the moonlight, then up and down and on, through the small hills, tired but now in sight of the fires and on into camp.

So then you sit, bundled against the evening chill, at the fire, with a whiskey and soda, waiting for the announcement that the canvas bath had been a quarter filled with hot water.

"*Bathi,* B'wana."

"God damn it, I could never hunt sheep again," you say. 58

"I never could," says P. O. M. "You all made me."

"You climbed a damn sight better than any of us."

"Do you suppose we could hunt sheep again, Pop?"

"I wonder," Pop said. "I suppose it's merely condition."

"It's riding in the damned cars that ruins us."

"If we did that walk every night we could come back in three nights from now and never feel it."

"Yes. But I'd be as scared of snakes if we did it every night for a year."

"You'd get over it."

"No," I said. "They scare me stiff. Do you remember that time we touched hands behind the tree?"

"Rather," said. Pop. "You jumped two yards. Are you really afraid of them, or only talking?"

"They scare me sick," I said. "They always have."

"What's the matter with you men?" P. O. M. said. "Why haven't I heard anything about the war tonight?"

"We're too bloody tired. Were you in the war, Pop?"

"Not me," said Pop. "Where is that boy with the whiskey?" Then calling in that feeble, clowning falsetto, "Kayti—Katy-ay!"

"*Bathi*," said Molo again softly, but insistently.

"Too tired."

"Memsahib *bathi*," Molo said hopefully.

"I'll go," said P. O. M. "But you two hurry up with your drinking. I'm hungry."

"*Bathi*," said Kayti severely to Pop.

"*Bathi* yourself," said Pop. "Don't bully me."

Kayti turned away in fire-lit slanting smile.

"All right. All right," said Pop. "Going to have one?" he asked.

"We'll have just one," I said, "and then we'll *bathi.*"

"*Bathi,* B'wana M'Kumba," Molo said. P. O. M. came toward the fire wearing her blue dressing gown and mosquito boots.

"Go on," she said. "You can have another when you come out. There's nice, warm, muddy water."

"They bully us," Pop said.

"Do you remember the time we were sheep hunting and your hat blew off and nearly fell onto the ram?" I asked her, the whiskey racing my mind back to Wyoming.

"Go take your bathi," P. O. M. said. "I'm going to have a gimlet."

In the morning we were dressed before daylight, ate breakfast, and were hunting the forest edge and the sunken valleys where Droop had seen the buffalo before the sun was up. But they were not there. It was a long hunt and we came back to camp and decided to send the trucks for porters and move with a foot safari to where there was supposed to be water in a stream that came down out of the mountain beyond where we had seen the rhinos the night before. Being camped there we could hunt a new country along the forest edge and we would be much closer to the mountain.

The trucks were to bring in Karl from his kudu camp where he seemed to be getting disgusted, or discouraged, or both, and he could go down to the Rift Valley the next day and kill some meat and try for an oryx. If we found good rhino we would send for him. We did not want to fire any shots where we were going except at rhino in order not to scare them, and we needed meat. The rhino seemed very shy and I knew from Wyoming how the shy game will all shift out of a small country, a country being an area, a valley or range of hills, a man can hunt in, after a shot or two. We planned this all out, Pop consulting with Droopy, and then sent the trucks off with Dan to recruit porters.

Late in the afternoon they were back with Karl, his outfit, and forty M'Bulus, good looking savages with a pompous headman who wore the only pair of shorts among them. Karl was thin now, his skin sallow, his eyes very tired looking and he seemed a little desperate. He had been eight days in the kudu camp in the hills, hunting hard, with no one with him who spoke any English, and they had only seen two cows and jumped a bull out of range. The guides claimed they had seen another bull but Karl had thought it was a kongoni, or that they said it was a kongoni, and had not shot. He was bitter about this and it was not a happy outfit.

"I never saw his horns. I don't believe it was a bull," he said. Kudu hunting was a touchy subject with him now and we let it alone.

"He'll get an oryx down there and he'll feel better," Pop said. "It's gotten on his nerves a little."

Karl agreed to the plan for us to move ahead into the new country and for him to go down for meat.

"Whatever you say," he said. "Absolutely whatever you say."

"It will give him some shooting," Pop said. "Then he'll feel better."

"We'll get one. Then you get one. Whoever gets his first can go on down after oryx. You'll probably get an oryx tomorrow anyway when you're hunting meat."

"Whatever you say," Karl said. His mind was bitterly revolving eight blank days of hill climbing in the heat, out before daylight, back at dark, hunting an animal whose Swahili name he could not then remember, with trackers in whom he had no confidence, coming back to eat alone, no one to whom he could talk, his wife nine thousand miles and three months away, and how was his dog and how was his job, and god-damn it where were they and what if he missed one when he got a shot, he wouldn't, you never missed when it was really important, he was sure of that, that was one of the tenets of his faith, but what if he got excited and missed, and why didn't he get any letters, what did the guide say kongoni for that time, they did, he knew they did, but he said nothing of all that, only, "Whatever you say," a little desperately.

"Come on, cheer up, you bastard," I said.

"I'm cheerful. What's the matter with you?"

"Have a drink."

"I don't want a drink. I want a god-damned kudu."

Later Pop said, "I thought he'd do well off by himself with no one to hurry him or rattle him. He'll be all right. He's a good lad."

"He wants some one to tell him exactly what to do and still leave him alone and not rattle him," I said. "It's hell for him to shoot in front of everybody. He's not a damned show-off like me."

"He made a damned fine shot at that leopard," Pop said.

"Two of them," I said. "The second was as good as the first. Hell, he can shoot. On the range he'll shoot the pants off of any of us. But he worries about it and I rattle him trying to get him to speed up."

"You're a little hard on him sometimes," Pop said.

"Hell, he knows me. He knows what I think of him. He doesn't mind."

"I still think he'll find himself off by himself," Pop said. "It's just a question of confidence. He's really a good shot."

"Hell, he's got the best buff, the best waterbuck, and the best lion, now," I said. "He's got nothing to worry about."

"The Memsahib has the best lion, brother. Don't make any mistake about that."

"I'm glad of that. But he's got a damned fine lion and

a big leopard. Everything he has is good. We've got plenty of time. He's got nothing to worry about. What the hell is he so gloomy about?"

"We'll get an early start in the morning so we can finish it off before it gets too hot for the little Memsahib."

"She's in the best shape of any one."

"She's marvellous. She's like a little terrier."

We went out that afternoon and glassed the country from the hills and never saw a thing. That night after supper we were in the tent. P. O. M. disliked intensely being compared to a little terrier. If she must be like any dog, and she did not wish to be, she would prefer a wolfhound, something lean, racy, long-legged and ornamental. Her courage was so automatic and so much a simple state of being that she never thought of danger; then, too, danger was in the hands of Pop and for Pop she had a complete, clear-seeing, absolutely trusting adoration. Pop was her ideal of how a man should be, brave, gentle, comic, never losing his temper, never bragging, never complaining except in a joke, tolerant, understanding, intelligent, drinking a little too much as a good man should, and, to her eyes, very handsome.

"Don't you think Pop's handsome?"

"No," I said. "Droopy's handsome."

"Droopy's *beautiful*. But don't you *really* think Pop's handsome?"

"Hell, no. I like him as well as any man I've ever known, but I'm damned if he's handsome."

"I think he's lovely looking. But you understand about how I feel about him, don't you?"

"Sure. I'm as fond of the bastard myself."

"But *don't* you think he's handsome, really?"

"Nope."

Then, a little later:

"Well, who's handsome to you?"

"Belmonte and Pop. And you."

"Don't be patriotic," I said. "Who's a beautiful woman?"

"Garbo."

"Not any more. Josie is. Margot is."

"Yes, they are. I know I'm not."

"You're lovely."

"Let's talk about Mr. J. P. I don't like you to call him Pop. It's not dignified."

"He and I aren't dignified together."

"Yes, but I'm dignified with him. Don't you think he's wonderful?"

"Yes, and he doesn't have to read books written by some female he's tried to help get published saying how he's yellow."

"She's just jealous and malicious. You never should have helped her. Some people never forgive that."

"It's a damned shame, though, with all that talent gone

to malice and nonsense and self-praise. It's a god-damned shame, really. It's a shame you never knew her before she went to pot. You know a funny thing; she never could write dialogue. It was terrible. She learned how to do it from my stuff and used it in that book. She had never written like that before. She never could forgive learning that and she was afraid people would notice it, where she'd learned it, so she had to attack me. It's a funny racket, really. But I swear she was damned nice before she got ambitious. You would have liked her then, really."

"Maybe, but I don't think so," said P. O. M. "We have fun though, don't we? Without all those people."

"God damn it if we don't. I've had a better time every year since I can remember."

"But isn't Mr. J. P. wonderful? Really?"

"Yes. He's wonderful."

"Oh, you're nice to say it. Poor Karl."

"Why?"

"Without his wife."

"Yes," I said. "Poor Karl."

CHAPTER

So in the morning, again, we started ahead of the porters and went down and across the hills and through
a deeply forested valley and then up and across a long
rise of country with high grass that made the walking
difficult and on and up and across, resting sometimes in
the shade of a tree, and then on and up and down and
across, all in high grass, now, that you had to break
a trail in, and the sun was very hot. The five of us in
single file, Droop and M'Cola with a big gun apiece,
hung with musettes and water bottles and the cameras,
we all sweating in the sun, Pop and I with guns and the
Memsahib trying to walk like Droopy, her Stetson tilted

FOUR

on one side, happy to be on a trip, pleased about how comfortable her boots were, we came finally to a thicket of thorn trees over a ravine that ran down from the side of a ridge to the water and we leaned the guns against the trees and went in under the close shade and lay on the ground. P. O. M. got the books out of one of the musettes and she and Pop read while I followed the ravine down to the little stream that came out of the mountain side, and found a fresh lion track and many rhino tunnels in the tall grass that came higher than your head. It was very hot climbing back up the sandy ravine and I was glad to lean my back against the tree trunk and read in Tolstoi's *Sevastopol*. It was a very young book and had one fine description of fighting in it, where the French take the redoubt and I thought about Tolstoi and about what a great advantage an experience of war was to a writer. It was one of the major subjects and certainly one of the hardest to write truly of and those writers who had not seen it were always very jealous and tried to make it seem unimportant, or abnormal, or a disease as a subject, while, really, it was just something quite irreplaceable that they had missed. Then Sevastopol made me think of the Boulevard Sevastopol in Paris, about riding a bicycle down it in the rain on the way home from Strassburg and the slipperiness of the rails of the tram cars and the feeling of riding on greasy, slippery asphalt and cobble stones in traffic in the rain, and how we had nearly lived on the Boulevard du Temple that time, and I remembered the look of that apartment, how it was arranged, and the wall paper, and instead we had taken the upstairs of the pavilion in Notre Dame des Champs in the courtyard with the sawmill (*and the sudden whine of the saw, the smell of sawdust and the chestnut tree over the roof with a mad woman downstairs*) and the year worrying about money (*all of the stories back in the mail that came in through a slit in the saw-mill door, with notes of rejection that would never call them stories, but always anecdotes, sketches, contes, etc. They did not want them, and we lived on poireaux and drank cahors and water*) and how fine the fountains were at the Place de L'Observatoire (*water sheen rippling on the bronze of horses' manes, bronze breasts and shoulders, green under thin-flowing water*) and when they put up the bust of Flaubert in the Luxembourg on the short cut through the gardens on the way to the rue Soufflot (*one that we believed in, loved without criticism, heavy now in stone as an idol should be*). He had not seen war but he had seen a revolution and the Commune and a revolution is much the best if you do not become bigoted because every one speaks the same language. Just as civil war is the best war for a writer, the most complete. Stendhal had seen a war and Napoleon taught him to write. He was teaching everybody then; but no one else learned. Dostoevsky was made by being sent to Siberia. Writers are forged in injustice as a sword is forged. I wondered if it would make a writer of him, give him the necessary shock to cut the over-flow of words and give him a sense of proportion, if they sent Tom Wolfe to Siberia or to the Dry Tortugas. Maybe it would and maybe it wouldn't. He seemed sad, really, like Carnera. Tolstoi was a small man. Joyce was of medium height and he wore his eyes out. And that last night, drunk, with Joyce and the thing he kept quoting from Edgar Quinet, "Fraîche et rose comme au jour de la bataille." I didn't have it right I knew. And when you saw him he would take up a conversation interrupted three years before. It was nice to see a great writer in our time.

What I had to do was work. I did not care, particularly, how it all came out. I did not take my own life seriously any more, any one else's life, yes, but not mine. They all wanted something that I did not want and I would get it without wanting it, if I worked. To work was the only thing, it was the one thing that always made you feel good, and in the meantime it was my own damned life and I would lead it where and how I pleased. And where I had led it now pleased me very much. This was a better sky than Italy. The hell it was. The best sky was in Italy and Spain and Northern Michigan in the fall and in the fall in the Gulf off Cuba. You could beat this sky; but not the country.

All I wanted to do now was get back to Africa. We had not left it, yet, but when I would wake in the night I would lie, listening, homesick for it already.

Now, looking out the tunnel of trees over the ravine at the sky with white clouds moving across in the wind, I loved the country so that I was happy as you are after you have been with a woman that you really love, when, empty, you feel it welling up again and there it is and you can never have it all and yet what there is, now, you can have, and you want more and more, to have, and be, and live in, to possess now again for always, for that long, sudden-ended always; making time stand still, sometimes so very still that afterwards you wait to hear it move, and it is slow in starting. But you are not alone, because if you have ever really loved her happy and un-

72

tragic, she loves you always; no matter whom she loves nor where she goes she loves you more. So if you have loved some woman and some country you are very fortunate and, if you die afterwards it makes no difference. Now, being in Africa, I was hungry for more of it, the changes of the seasons, the rains with no need to travel, the discomforts that you paid to make it real, the names of the trees, of the small animals, and all the birds, to know the language and have time to be in it and to move slowly. I had loved country all my life; the country was always better than the people. I could only care about people a very few at a time.

P. O. M. was sleeping. She was always lovely to look at asleep, sleeping quietly, close curled like an animal, with nothing of the being dead look that Karl had asleep. Pop slept quietly too, you could see his soul was close in his body. His body no longer housed him fittingly. It had gone on and changed, thickening here, losing its lines, bloating a little there, but inside he was young and lean and tall and hard as when he galloped lion on the plain below Wami, and the pouches under his eyes were all outside, so that now I saw him asleep the way P. O. M. saw him always. M'Cola was an old man asleep, without history and without mystery. Droopy did not sleep. He sat on his heels and watched for the safari.

We saw them coming a long way off. At first the boxes just showed above the high grass, then a line of heads, then they were in a hollow, and there was only the point of a spear in the sun, then they came up a rise of ground and I could see the strung out line coming toward us. They had gone a little too far to the left and Droopy waved to signal them toward us. They made camp, Pop warning them to be quiet, and we sat under the dining tent and were comfortable in the chairs and talked. That night we hunted and saw nothing. The next morning we hunted and saw nothing and the next evening the same. It was very interesting but there were no results. The wind blew hard from the east and the ground was broken in short ridges of hills coming down close from the forest so you could not get above it without sending your scent on ahead of you on the wind to warn everything. You could not see into the sun in the evening, nor on the heavy shadowed hillsides to the west, beyond which the sun was setting at the time the rhino would be coming out of the forest; so all the country to the westward was a loss in the evening and in the country we could hunt we found nothing. Meat came in from Karl's camp by some porters we sent back. They came in carrying quarters of tommy, Grant, and wildebeeste, dusty, the meat seared dry by the sun, and the porters were happy, crouched around their fires roasting the meat on sticks. Pop was puzzled why the rhino were all gone. Each day we had seen less and we discussed whether it could be the full moon, that they fed out at night and were back in the forest in the morning before it was light, or that they winded us, or heard the men, and were simply shy and kept in the forest, or what was it? Me putting out the theories, Pop pricking them with his wit, sometimes considering them from politeness, sometimes with interest, like the one about the moon.

We went to bed early and in the night it rained a little, not a real rain but a shower from the mountains, and in the morning we were up before daylight and had climbed up to the top of the steep grassy ridge that looked down onto the camp, onto the ravine of the river bed, and across to the steep opposite bank of the stream, and from where we could see all the hilly slopes and the edge of the forest. It was not yet light when some geese flew overhead and the light was still too gray to be able to see the edge of the forest clearly in the glasses. We had scouts out on three different hill tops and we were waiting for it to be light enough for us to see them if they signalled.

Then Pop said, "Look at that son of a bitch," and shouted at M'Cola to bring the rifles. M'Cola went jumping down the hill, and across the stream, directly opposite us, a rhino was running with a quick trot along the top of the bank. As we watched he speeded up and came, fast trotting, angling down across the face of the bank. He was a muddy red, his horn showed clearly, and there was nothing ponderous in his quick, purposeful movement. I was very excited at seeing him.

"He'll cross the stream," Pop said. "He's shootable."

M'Cola put the Springfield in my hand and I opened it to make sure I had solids. The rhino was out of sight now but I could see the shaking of the high grass.

"How far would you call it?"

"All of three hundred."

"I'll bust the son of a bitch."

I was watching, freezing myself deliberately inside, stopping the excitement as you close a valve, going into that impersonal state you shoot from.

He showed, trotting into the shallow, boulder filled stream. Thinking of one thing, that the shot was perfectly possible, but that I must lead him enough, must get ahead, I got on him, then well ahead of him, and squeezed off. I heard the *whonk* of the bullet and, from his trot, he seemed to explode forward. With a whooshing snort he smashed ahead, splashing water and snorting. I shot again and raised a little column of water behind him, and shot again as he went into the grass; behind him again.

"Piga," M'Cola said. "Piga!"

Droopy agreed.

"Did you hit him?" Pop said.

"Absolutely," I said. "I think I've got him."

Droopy was running and I re-loaded and ran off after him. Half the camp was strung out across the hills waving and yelling. The rhino had come in right below where they were and gone on up the valley toward where the forest came close down into the head of the valley.

Pop and P. O. M. came up. Pop with his big gun and M'Cola carrying mine.

"Droopy will get the tracks," Pop said. "M'Cola swears you hit him."

"Piga!" M'Cola said.

"He snorted like a steam engine," P. O. M. said. "Didn't he look wonderful going along there?"

"He was late getting home with the milk," Pop said. "Are you *sure* you hit him? It was a godawful long shot."

"I *know* I hit him. I'm *pretty* sure I've killed him."

"Don't tell any one if you did," Pop said. "They'll never believe you. Look! Droopy's got blood."

Below, in the high grass Droop was holding up a grass blade toward us. Then, stooped, he went on trailing fast by the blood spoor.

"Piga," M'Cola said. "M'uzuri!"

"We'll keep up above where we can see if he makes a break," Pop said. "Look at Droopy."

Droop had removed his fez and held it in his hand.

"That's all the precautions he needs," Pop said. "We bring up a couple of heavy guns and Droopy goes in after him with one article less of clothing."

Below us Droopy and his partner who was trailing with him had stopped. Droopy held up his hand.

"They hear him," Pop said. "Come on."

We started toward them. Droopy came toward us and spoke to Pop.

"He's in there," Pop whispered. "They can hear the tick birds. One of the boys says he heard the faro, too. We'll go in against the wind. You go ahead with Droopy. Let the Memsahib stay behind me. Take the big gun. All right."

The rhino was in high grass, somewhere in there behind some bushes. As we went forward we heard a deep, moaning sort of groan. Droopy looked around at me and grinned. The noise came again, ending this time like a blood-choked sigh. Droopy was laughing. "Faro," he whispered and put his hand palm open on the side of his head in the gesture that means to go to sleep. Then in a jerky-flighted, sharp-beaked little flock we saw the tick birds rise and fly away. We knew where he was and, as we went slowly forward, parting the high grass, we saw him. He was on his side, dead.

"Better shoot him once to make sure," Pop said. M'Cola handed me the Springfield he had been carrying. I noticed it was cocked, looked at M'Cola, furious with him, kneeled down and shot the rhino in the sticking place. He never moved. Droopy shook my hand and so did M'Cola.

"He had that damned Springfield cocked," I said to Pop. The cocked gun, behind my back, made me black angry.

That meant nothing to M'Cola. He was very happy, stroking the rhino's horn, measuring it with his fingers spread, looking for the bullet hole.

"It's on the side he's lying on," I said.

"You should have seen him when he was protecting Mama," Pop said. "That's why he had the gun cocked."

"Can he shoot?"

"No," Pop said. "But he would."

"Shoot me in the pants," I said. "Romantic bastard." When the whole outfit came up, we rolled the rhino into a sort of kneeling position and cut away the grass to take some pictures. The bullet hole was fairly high in the back, a little behind the lungs.

"That was a hell of a shot," Pop said. "A hell of a shot. Don't ever tell any one you made that one."

"You'll have to give me a certificate."

"That would just make us both liars. They're a strange beast, aren't they?"

There he was, long-hulked, heavy-sided, prehistoric looking, the hide like vulcanized rubber and faintly transparent looking, scarred with a badly healed horn wound that the birds had pecked at, his tail thick, round, and pointed, flat many-legged ticks crawling on him, his ears fringed with hair, tiny pig eyes, moss growing on the base of his horn that grew out forward from his nose. M'Cola looked at him and shook his head. I agreed with him. This was the hell of an animal.

"How is his horn?"

"It isn't bad," Pop said. "It's nothing extra. That was a hell of a shot you made on him though, brother."

"M'Cola's pleased with it," I said.

79

"You're pretty pleased with it yourself," P. O. M. said.

"I'm crazy about it," I said. "But don't let me start on it. Don't worry about how I feel about it. I can wake up and think about that any night."

"And you're a good tracker, and a hell of a fine bird shot, too," Pop said. "Tell us the rest of that."

"Lay off me. I only said that once when I was drunk."

"Once," said P. O. M. "Doesn't he tell us that every night?"

"By God, I *am* a good bird shot."

"Amazing," said Pop. "I never would have thought it. What else is it you do?"

"Oh, go to hell."

"Musn't ever let him realize what a shot that was or he'll get unbearable," Pop said to P. O. M.

"M'Cola and I know," I said.

M'Cola came up. "M'uzuri, B'wana," he said. "M'uzuri sana."

"He thinks you did it on purpose," Pop said.

"Don't you ever tell him different."

"Piga m'uzuri," M'Cola said. "M'uzuri."

"I believe he feels just the way you do about it," Pop said.

"He's my pal."

"I believe he is, you know," Pop said.

On our way back across country to our main camp I made a fancy shot on a reedbuck at about two hundred yards, offhand, breaking his neck at the base of the skull. M'Cola was very pleased and Droopy was delighted.

"We've got to put a stop to him," Pop said to P. O. M. "Where did you shoot for, really?"

"In the neck," I lied. I had held full on the center of the shoulder.

"It was awfully pretty," P. O. M. said. The bullet had made a crack when it hit like a baseball bat swung against a fast ball and the buck had collapsed without a move.

"I think he's a damned liar," Pop said.

"None of us great shots is appreciated. Wait till we're gone."

"His idea of being appreciated is for us to carry him on our shoulders," Pop said. "That rhino shot has ruined him."

"All right. You watch from now on. Hell, I've shot well the whole time."

"I seem to remember a Grant of some sort," Pop was teasing. So did I remember him. I'd followed a fine one out of the country missing shot after shot all morning after a series of stalks in the heat, then crawled up to an ant hill to shoot one that was not nearly as good, taken a rest on the ant hill, missed the buck at fifty yards, seen him stand facing me, absolutely still, his nose up, and shot him in the chest. He went over backwards and as I went up to him he jumped up and went off, staggering. I sat down and waited for him to stop and when he did, obviously anchored, I sat there, using the sling, and shot for his neck, slowly and carefully, missing him eight times straight in a mounting, stubborn rage, not making a correction but shooting exactly for the same place in the same way each time, the gun bearers all laughing, the truck that had come up with the outfit holding more amused niggers, P. O. M. and Pop saying nothing, me sitting there cold, crazy-stubborn-furious, determined to break his neck rather than walk up and perhaps start him off over that heat-hazy, baking, noontime plain. Nobody said anything. I reached up my hand to M'Cola for more cartridges, shot again, carefully, and missed, and on the tenth shot broke his damned neck. I turned away without looking toward him.

"Poor Papa," P. O. M. said.

"It's the light and the wind," Pop said. We had not known each other very well then. "They were all hitting the same place. I could see them throw the dust."

"I was a damned bloody stubborn fool," I said.

Anyway, I could shoot now. So far, and aided by flukes, my luck was running now.

We came on into sight of camp and shouted. No one came out. Finally Karl came out of his tent. He went back in as soon as he saw us, then came out again.

"Hey, Karl," I yelled. He waved and went back in the tent again. Then came toward us. He was shaky with excitement and I saw he had been washing blood off his hands.

"What is it?"

"Rhino," he said.

"Did you get in trouble with him?"

"No. We killed him."

"Fine. Where is he?"

"Over there behind that tree."

We went over. There was the newly severed head of a rhino that was a rhino. He was twice the size of the one I had killed. The little eyes were shut and a fresh drop of blood stood in the corner of one like a tear. The head bulked enormous and the horn swept up and back in a fine curve. The hide was an inch thick where it hung in a cape behind the head and was as white where it was cut as freshly sliced coconut.

"What is he? About thirty inches?"

"Hell, no," said Pop. "No thirty inches."

"But he iss a very fine one, Mr. Jackson," Dan said.

"Yes. He's a fine one," Pop said.

"Where did you get him?"

"Just outside of camp."

"He wass standing in some bush. We heard him grunt."

"We thought he was a buffalo," Karl said.

"He iss a very fine one," Dan repeated.

"I'm damned glad you got him," I said.

There we were, the three of us, wanting to congratulate, waiting to be good sports about this rhino whose smaller horn was longer than our big one, this huge, tear-eyed marvel of a rhino, this dead, head-severed dream rhino, and instead we all spoke like people who were about to become seasick on a boat, or people who had suffered some heavy financial loss. We were ashamed and could do nothing about it. I wanted to say something pleasant and hearty, instead, "How many times did you shoot him?" I asked.

"I don't know. We didn't count. Five or six, I guess."

"Five, I think," said Dan.

Poor Karl, faced by these three sad-faced congratulators, was beginning to feel his pleasure in the rhino drained away from him.

"We got one too," said P. O. M.

"That's fine," said Karl. "Is he bigger than this one?"

"Hell, no. He's a lousy runt."

"I'm sorry," Karl said. He meant it, simply and truly.

"What the hell have you got to be sorry about with a rhino like that? Goddamn it, he's a beauty. Let me get the camera and take some pictures of him."

I went after the camera. P. O. M. took me by the arm and walked close beside me.

"Papa, please try to act like a human being," she said. "Poor Karl. You're making him feel dreadfully."

"I know it," I said. "I'm trying not to act that way."

There was Pop. He shook his head. "I never felt more of a four-letter man," he said. "But it was like a kick in the stomach. I'm really delighted, of course."

"Me too," I said. "I'd rather have him beat me. You

84

know that. Truly. But why couldn't he just get a good one, two or three inches longer? Why did he have to get one that makes mine ridiculous? It just makes ours silly."

"You can always remember that shot."

"The hell with that shot. That bloody fluke. God, what a beautiful rhino."

"Come on, let's pull ourselves together and try to act like white people with him."

"We were *awful*," P. O. M. said.

"I know it," I said. "And all the time I was trying to be jolly. You *know* I'm delighted he has it."

"You were certainly jolly. Both of you," P. O. M. said.

"But did you see M'Cola?" Pop asked. M'Cola had looked at the rhino dismally, shaken his head and walked away.

"He's a wonderful rhino," P. O. M. said. "We must act decently and make Karl feel good."

But it was too late. We could not make Karl feel good and for a long time we could not feel good ourselves. The porters came into camp with the loads and we could see them all, and all of our outfit, go over to where the rhino head lay in the shade. They were all very quiet. Only the skinner was delighted to see such a rhino head in camp.

"M'uzuri sana," he said to me. And measured the horn with shiftings of his widespread hand. "Kubwa sana!"

85

"N'Dio. M'uzuri sana," I agreed.

"B'wana Kabor shoot him?"

"Yes."

"M'uzuri sana."

"Yes," I agreed. "M'uzuri sana."

The skinner was the only gent in the outfit. We had tried, in all the shoot, never to be competitive. Karl and I had each tried to give the other the better chance on everything that came up. I was, truly, very fond of him and he was entirely unselfish and altogether self-sacrificing. I knew I could outshoot him and I could always outwalk him and, steadily, he got trophies that made mine dwarfs in comparison. He had done some of the worst shooting at game I had ever seen and I had shot badly twice on the trip, at that Grant, and at a bustard once on the plain, still he beat me on all the tangible things we had to show. For a while we had joked about it 'and I knew everything would even up. But it didn't even up. Now, on this rhino hunt, I had taken the first crack at the country. We had sent him after meat while we had gone into a new country. We had not treated him badly, but we had not treated him too well, and still he had beaten me. Not only beaten, beaten was all right. He had made my rhino look so small that I could never keep him in the same small town where we lived. He had wiped him out. I had the shot I had made on him to remember and nothing could take that away except that it was so bloody marvellous I knew I would wonder, sooner or later, if it was not really a fluke in spite of my unholy self-confidence. Old Karl had put it on us all right with that rhino. He was in his tent now, writing a letter.

Under the dining tent fly Pop and I talked over what we had better do.

"He's got his rhino anyway," Pop said. "That saves us time. Now you can't stand on that one."

"No."

"But this country is washed out. Something wrong with it. Droopy claims to know a good country about three hours from here in the trucks and another hour or so in with the porters. We can head for there this afternoon with a light outfit, send the trucks back, and Karl and Dan can move on down to M'uto Umbu and he can get his oryx."

"Fine."

"He has a chance to get a leopard on that rhino carcass this evening, too, or in the morning. Dan said they heard one. We'll try to get a rhino out of this country of Droopy's and then you join up with them and go on for kudu. We want to leave plenty of time for them."

"Fine."

"Even if you don't get an oryx. You'll pick one up somewhere."

"Even if I don't get one at all, it's all right. We'll get one another time. I want a kudu, though."

"You'll get one. You're sure to."

"I'd rather get one, a good one, than all the rest. I don't give a damn about these rhino outside of the fun of hunting them. But I'd like to get one that wouldn't look silly beside that dream rhino of his."

"Absolutely."

So we told Karl and he said: "Whatever you say. Sure. I hope you get one twice as big." He really meant it. He was feeling better now and so were we all.

CHAPTER

Droopy's country, when we reached it that evening, after a hot ride through red-soiled, bush-scrubby hills, looked awful. It was at the edge of a belt where all the trees had been girdled to kill the tse-tse flies. And across from camp was a dusty, dirty native village. The soil was red and eroded and seemed to be blowing away and camp was pitched in a high wind under the sketchy shade of some dead trees on a hillside overlooking a little stream and the mud village beyond. Before dark we followed Droopy and two local guides up past the village and in a long climb to the top of a rock-strewn ridge that overlooked a deep valley that was almost a canyon. Across, on the other side, were broken valleys that sloped

FIVE

steeply down into the canyon. There were heavy growths of trees in the valleys and grassy slopes on the ridges between, and above there was the thick bamboo forest of the mountain. The canyon ran down to the Rift Valley, seeming to narrow at the far end where it cut through the wall of the rift. Beyond, above the grassy ridges and slopes, were heavily forested hills. It looked a hell of a country to hunt.

"If you see one across there you have to go straight down to the bottom of the canyon. Then up one of those timber patches and across those damned gullies. You can't keep him in sight and you'll kill yourself climbing. It's too bloody steep. Those are the kind of innocent-looking gullies we got into that night coming home."

"It looks very bad," Pop agreed.

"I've hunted a country just like this for deer. The south slope of Timber Creek in Wyoming. The slopes are all too steep. It's hell. It's too broken. We'll take some punishment tomorrow."

P. O. M. said nothing. Pop had brought us here and Pop would bring us out. All she had to do was see her shoes did not hurt her feet. They hurt just a little now, and that was her only worry.

I went on to dilate on the difficulties the country showed and we went home to camp in the dark all very gloomy and full of prejudice against Droopy. The fire flamed brightly in the wind and we sat and watched the moon rise and listened to the hyenas. After we had a few drinks we did not feel so badly about the country.

"Droopy swears it's good," Pop said. "This isn't where he wanted to go though, he says. It was another place further on. But he swears this is good."

"I love Droopy," P. O. M. said. "I have perfect confidence in Droopy."

Droopy came up to the fire with two spear-carrying natives.

"What does he hear?" I asked.

There was some talk by the natives, then Pop said: "One of these sportsmen claims he was chased by a huge rhino today. Of course nearly any rhino would look huge when he was chasing him."

"Ask him how long the horn was."

The native showed that the horn was as long as his arm. Droopy grinned.

"Tell him to go," said Pop.

"Where did all this happen?"

"Oh, over there somewhere," Pop said. "You know. Over there. Way over there. Where these things always happen."

"That's marvellous. Just where we want to go."

"The good aspect is that Droopy's not at all depressed," Pop said. "He seems very confident. After all, it's his show."

"Yes, but we have to do the climbing."

"Cheer him up, will you?" Pop said to P. O. M. "He's getting me very depressed."

"Should we talk about how well he shoots?"

"Too bloody early in the evening. I'm not gloomy. I've just seen that kind of country before. It will be good for us all right. Take some of your belly off, Governor."

The next day I found that I was all wrong about that country.

WE had breakfast before daylight and were started before sunrise, climbing the hill beyond the village in single file. Ahead there was the local guide with a spear, then Droopy with my heavy gun and a water bottle, then me with the Springfield, Pop with the Mannlicher, P. O.

M. pleased, as always, to carry nothing, M'Cola with Pop's heavy gun and another water bottle, and finally two local citizens with spears, water bags, and a chop box with lunch. We planned to lay up in the heat of the middle of the day and not get back until dark. It was fine climbing in the cool fresh morning and very different from toiling up this same trail last evening in the sunset with all the rocks and dirt giving back the heat of the day. The trail was used regularly by cattle and the dust was powdered dry and, now, lightly moistened from the dew. There were many hyena tracks and, as the trail came onto a ridge of gray rock so that you could look down on both sides into a steep ravine, and then went on along the edge of the canyon, we saw a fresh rhino track in one of the dusty patches below the rocks.

"He's just gone on ahead," Pop said. "They must wander all over here at night."

Below, at the bottom of the canyon, we could see the tops of high trees and in an opening see the flash of water. Across were the steep hillside and the gullies we had studied last night. Droopy and the local guide, the one who had been chased by the rhino, were whispering together. Then they started down a steep path that went in long slants down the side of the canyon.

We stopped. I had not seen P. O. M. was limping, and in sudden whispered family bitterness there was a highly-righteous-on-both-sides clash, historically on unwearable shoes and boots in the past, and imperatively on these, which hurt. The hurt was lessened by cutting off the toes of the heavy short wool socks worn over ordinary socks, and then, by removing the socks entirely, the boots made possible. Going down-hill steeply made these Spanish shooting boots too short in the toe and there was an old argument, about this length of boot and whether the bootmaker, whose part I had taken, unwittingly first, only as interpreter, and finally embraced his theory patriotically as a whole and, I believed, by logic, had overcome it by adding onto the heel. But they hurt now, a stronger logic, and the situation was un-helped by the statement that men's new boots always hurt for weeks before they became comfortable. Now, heavy socks removed, stepping tentatively, trying the pressure of the leather against the toes, the argument past, she wanting not to suffer, but to keep up and please Mr. J. P., me ashamed at having been a four-letter man about boots, at being righteous against pain, at being righteous at all, at ever being righteous, stopping to whisper about it, both of us grinning at what was whispered, it all right now, the boots too, without the heavy socks, much better, me hating all righteous bastards now, one absent American friend especially, having just removed myself from that category, certainly never to be righteous again, watching Droopy ahead, we went down the long slant of the trail toward the bottom of the canyon where the trees were heavy and tall and the floor of the canyon, that from above had been a narrow gash, opened to a forest-banked stream.

95

We stood now in the shade of trees with great smooth trunks, circled at their base with the line of roots that showed in rounded ridges up the trunks like arteries; the trunks the yellow green of a French forest on a day in winter after rain. But these trees had a great spread of branches and were in leaf and below them, in the stream bed in the sun, reeds like papyrus grass grew thick as wheat and twelve feet tall. There was a game trail through the grass along the stream and Droopy was bent down looking at it. M'Cola went over and looked and they both followed it a little way, stooped close over it, then came back to us.

"Nyati," M'Cola whispered. "Buffalo." Droopy whispered to Pop and then Pop said, softly in his throaty, whiskey whisper, "They're buff gone down the river. Droop says there are some big bulls. They haven't come back."

"Let's follow them," I said. "I'd rather get another buff than rhino."

"It's as good a chance as any for rhino, too," Pop said.

"By God, isn't it a great looking country?" I said.

"Splendid," Pop said. "Who would have imagined it?"

"The trees are like André's pictures," P. O. M. said. "It's simply beautiful. Look at that green. It's Masson. Why can't a good painter see this country?"

"How are your boots?"

"Fine."

As we trailed the buffalo we went very slowly and

quietly. There was no wind and we knew that when the breeze came up it would be from the east and blow up the canyon toward us. We followed the game trail down the river-bed and as we went the grass was much higher. Twice we had to get down to crawl and the reeds were so thick you could not see two feet into them. Droop found a fresh rhino track, too, in the mud. I began to think about what would happen if a rhino came barging along this tunnel and who would do what. It was exciting but I did not like it. It was too much like being in a trap and there was P. O. M. to think about. Then as the stream made a bend and we came out of the high grass to the bank I smelled game very distinctly. I do not smoke, and hunting at home I have several times smelled elk in the rutting season before I have seen them and I can smell clearly where an old bull has lain in the forest. The bull elk has a strong musky smell. It is a strong but pleasant odor and I know it well, but this smell I did not know.

"I can smell them," I whispered to Pop. He believed me.

"What is it?"

"I don't know but it's plenty strong. Can't you?"

"No."

"Ask Droop."

Droopy nodded and grinned.

"They take snuff," Pop said. "I don't know whether they can scent or not."

We went on into another bed of reeds that were high over our heads, putting each foot down silently before lifting the other, walking as quietly as in a dream or a slow motion picture. I could smell whatever it was clearly now, all of the time, sometimes stronger than at others. I did not like it at all. We were close to the bank now, and, ahead the game trail went straight out into a long slough of higher reeds than any we had come through.

"I can smell them close as hell," I whispered to Pop. "No kidding. Really."

"I believe you," Pop said. "Should we get up here onto the bank and skirt this bit? We'll be above it."

"Good." Then, when we were up, I said, "That tall stuff had me spooked. I wouldn't like to hunt in that."

"How'd you like to hunt elephant in that?" Pop whispered.

"I wouldn't do it."

"Do you really hunt elephant in grass like that?" P. O. M. asked.

"Yes," Pop said. "Get up on somebody's shoulders to shoot."

Better men than I am do it, I thought. I wouldn't do it.

We went along the grassy right bank, on a sort of shelf, now in the open, skirting a slough of high dry reeds. Beyond on the opposite bank were the heavy trees and above them the steep bank of the canyon. You could not see the stream. Above us, on the right, were the hills, wooded in patches of orchard bush. Ahead, at the end of the slough of reeds the banks narrowed and the branches of the big trees almost covered the stream. Suddenly Droopy grabbed me and we both crouched down. He put the big gun in my hand and took the Springfield. He pointed and around a curve in the bank I saw the head of a rhino with a long, wonderful-looking horn. The head was swaying and I could see the ears forward and twitching, and see the little pig eyes. I slipped the safety catch and motioned Droopy down. Then I heard M'Cola saying, "Toto! Toto!" and he grabbed my arm. Droopy was whispering, "Manamouki! Manamouki! Manamouki!" very fast and he and M'Cola were frantic that I should not shoot. It was a cow rhino with a calf and as I lowered the gun, she gave a snort, crashed in the reeds, and was gone. I never saw the calf. We could see the reeds swaying where the two of them were moving and then it was all quiet.

"Damn shame," Pop whispered. "She had a beautiful horn."

"I was all set to bust her," I said. "I couldn't tell she was a cow."

"M'Cola saw the calf."

M'Cola was whispering to Pop and nodding his head emphatically.

"He says there's another rhino in there," Pop said. "That he heard him snort."

"Let's get higher, where we can see them if they break, and throw something in," I said.

"Good idea," Pop agreed. "Maybe the bull's there."

We went a little higher up the bank where we could look out over the lake of high reeds and, with Pop holding his big gun ready and I with the safety off mine, M'Cola threw a club into the reeds where he had heard the snort. There was a wooshing snort and no movement, not a stir in the reeds. Then there was a crashing further away and we could see the reeds swaying with the rush of something through them toward the opposite bank, but could not see what was making the movement. Then I saw the black back, the wide-swept, point-lifted horns and then the quick-moving, climbing rush of a buffalo up the other bank. He went up, his neck up and out, his head horn-heavy, his withers rounded like a fighting bull, in fast strong-legged climb. I was holding on the point where his neck joined his shoulder when Pop stopped me.

"He's not a big one," he said softly. "I wouldn't take him unless you want him for meat."

He looked big to me and now he stood, his head up, broadside, his head swung toward us.

"I've got three more on the license and we're leaving their country," I said.

"It's awfully good meat," Pop whispered. "Go ahead then. Bust him. But be ready for the rhino after you shoot."

I sat down, the big gun feeling heavy and unfamiliar, held on the buff's shoulder, squeezed off and flinched without firing. Instead of the sweet clean pull of the Springfield with the smooth, unhesitant release at the end, this trigger came to what, in a squeeze, seemed metal stuck against metal. It was like when you shoot in a nightmare. I couldn't squeeze it and I corrected from my flinch, held my breath, and pulled the trigger. It pulled off with a jerk and the big gun made a rocking explosion out of which I came, seeing the buffalo still on his feet, and going out of sight to the left in a climbing run, to let off the second barrel and throw a burst of rock dust and dirt over his hind quarters. He was out of shot before I could reload the double-barrelled .470 and we had all heard the snorting and the crashing of another rhino that had gone out of the lower end of the reeds and on under the heavy trees on our side without showing more than a glimpse of his bulk in the reeds.

"It was the bull," Pop said. "He's gone down the stream."

"N'Dio. Doumi! Doumi!" Droopy insisted it was a bull.

"I hit the damned buff," I said. "God knows where. To hell with those heavy guns. The trigger pull put me off."

"You'd have killed him with the Springfield," Pop said.

"I'd know where I hit him anyway. I thought with the four-seventy I'd kill him or miss him," I said. "Instead, now we've got him wounded."

"He'll keep," Pop said. "We want to give him plenty of time."

"I'm afraid I gut-shot him."

"You can't tell. Going off fast like that he might be dead in a hundred yards."

"The hell with that four-seventy," I said. "I can't shoot it. The trigger's like the last turn of the key opening a sardine can."

"Come on," Pop said. "We've got God knows how many rhino scattered about here."

"What about the buff?"

"Plenty of time for him later. We must let him stiffen up. Let him get sick."

"Suppose we'd been down in there with all that stuff coming out."

"Yes," said Pop.

All this in whispers. I looked at P. O. M. She was like some one enjoying a good musical show.

"Did you see where it hit him?"

"I couldn't tell," she whispered. "Do you suppose there are any more in there?"

"Thousands," I said. "What do we do, Pop?"

"That bull may be just around the bend," Pop said. "Come on."

We went along the bank, our nerves cocked, and as we came to the narrow end of the reeds there was another rush of something heavy through the tall stalks. I had the gun up waiting for whatever it was to show. But there was only the waving of the reeds. M'Cola signalled with his hand not to shoot.

"The goddamned calf," Pop said. "Must have been two of them. Where's the bloody bull?"

"How the hell do you see them?"

"Tell by the size."

Then we were standing looking down into the stream bed, into the shadows under the branches of the big trees, and off ahead down the stream when M'Cola pointed up the hill on our right.

"Faro," he whispered and reached me the glasses.

There on the hillside, head-on, wide, black, looking straight toward us, ears twitching and head lifted, swaying as the nose searched for the wind, was another rhino. He looked huge in the glasses. Pop was studying him with his binoculars.

"He's no better than what you have," he said softly.

"I can bust him right in the sticking place," I whispered.

"You only have one more," Pop whispered. "You want a good one."

I offered the glasses to P. O. M.

"I can see him without," she said. "He's huge."

"He may charge," Pop said. "Then you'll have to take him."

Then, as we watched, another rhino came into sight from behind a wide feathery-topped tree. He was quite a bit smaller.

"By God, it's a calf," Pop said. "That one's a cow. Good thing you didn't shoot her. She bloody well *may* charge too."

"Is it the same cow?" I whispered.

"No. That other one had a hell of a horn."

We all had the nervous exhilaration, like a laughing drunk, that a sudden over-abundance, idiotic abundance of game makes. It is a feeling that can come from any sort of game or fish that is ordinarily rare and that, suddenly, you find in a ridiculously unbelievable abundance.

"Look at her. She knows there's something wrong. But she can't see us or smell us."

"She heard the shots."

"She knows we're here. But she can't make it out."

The rhino looked so huge, so ridiculous, and so fine to see, and I sighted on her chest.

"It's a nice shot."

"Perfect," Pop said.

"What are we going to do?" P. O. M. said. She was practical.

"We'll work around her," Pop said.

"If we keep low I don't believe our scent will carry up there once we're past."

"You can't tell," Pop said. "We don't want her to charge."

She did not charge, but dropped her head, finally, and worked up the hill followed by the nearly full-grown calf.

"Now," said Pop, "we'll let Droop go ahead and see if he can find the bull's tracks. We might as well sit down."

We sat in the shade and Droopy went up one side of the stream and the local guide the other. They came back and said the bull had gone on down.

"Did any one ever see what sort of horn he had?" I asked.

"Droop said he was good."

M'Cola had gone up the hill a little way. Now he crouched and beckoned.

"Nyati," he said with his hand up to his face.

"Where?" Pop asked him. He pointed, crouched down, and as we crawled up to him he handed me the glasses. They were a long way away on the jutting ridge of one of the steep hillsides on the far side of the canyon, well down the stream. We could see six, then eight, buffalo, black, heavy necked, the horns shining, standing on the point of a ridge. Some were grazing and others stood, their heads up, watching.

"That one's a bull," Pop said, looking through the glasses.

"Which one?"

"Second from the right."

"They all look like bulls to me."

"They're a long way away. That one's a good bull. Now we've got to cross the stream and work down toward them and try to get above them."

"Will they stay there?"

"No. Probably they'll work down into this stream bed as soon as it's hot."

"Let's go."

We crossed the stream on a log and then another log and on the other side, half way up the hillside, there was a deeply worn game trail that graded along the bank under the heavily leafed branches of the trees. We went along quite fast, but walking carefully, and below us, now, the stream bed was covered solidly with foliage. It was still early in the morning but the breeze was rising and the leaves stirred over our heads. We crossed one ravine that came down to the stream, going into the thick bush to be out of sight and stooping as we crossed behind trees in the small open place, then, using the shoulder of the ravine as protection, we climbed so that we might get high up the hillside above the buffalo and work down to them. We stopped in the shelter of the ridge, me sweating heavily and fixing a handkerchief inside the sweatband of my Stetson, and sent Droop ahead to look. He came back to say they were gone. From above we could see nothing of them, so we cut across the ravine and the hillside thinking we might intercept them on their way down into the river bed. The next hillside had been burned and at the bottom of the hill there was a burned area of bush. In the ash dust were the tracks of the buffalo as they came down and into the thick jungle of the stream bed. Here it was too overgrown and there were too many vines to follow them. There were no tracks going down the stream so we knew they were down in that part of the stream bed we had looked down on from the game trail. Pop said there was nothing to do about them in there. It was so thick that if we jumped them we could not get a shot. You could not tell one from another, he said. All you would see would be a rush of black. An old bull would be gray but a good herd bull might be as black as a cow. It wasn't any good to jump them like that.

It was ten o'clock now and very hot in the open, the sun pegged and the breeze lifted the ashes of the burned-over ground as we walked. Everything would be in the thick cover now. We decided to find a shady place and lie down and read in the cool; to have lunch and kill the hot part of the day.

Beyond the burned place we came toward the stream and stopped, sweating, in the shadow of some very large trees. We unpacked our leather coats and our raincoats and spread them on the grass at the foot of the trees so that we could lean back against the trunks. P. O. M. got out the books and M'Cola made a small fire and boiled water for tea.

The breeze was coming up and we could hear it in the high branches. It was cool in the shade, but if you stirred into the sun, or as the sun shifted the shadow while you read so that any part of you was out of the shadow, the sun was heavy. Droopy had gone on down the stream to have a look and as we lay there, reading, I could smell the heat of the day coming, the drying up of the dew, the heat on the leaves, and the heaviness of the sun over the stream.

P. O. M. was reading *Spanish Gold,* by George A. Birmingham, and she said it was no good. I still had the Sevastopol book of Tolstoi and in the same volume I was reading a story called "The Cossacks" that was very good. In it were the summer heat, the mosquitoes, the feel of the forest in the different seasons, and that river that the Tartars crossed, raiding, and I was living in that Russia again.

I was thinking how real that Russia of the time of our Civil War was, as real as any other place, as Michigan, or the prairie north of town and the woods around Evans's game farm, of how, through Turgenieff, I knew that I had lived there, as I had been in the family Buddenbrooks, and had climbed in and out of her window in *Le Rouge et Le Noir,* or the morning we had come in the gates of Paris and seen Salcède torn apart by the horses at the Place de Grèves. I saw all that. And it was me they did not break on the rack that time because I had been polite to the executioner the time they killed Coconas and me, and I remember the Eve of St. Bartholomew's and how we hunted Huguenots that night, and when they trapped me at her house that time, and no feeling more true than finding the gate of the Louvre being closed, nor of looking down at his body in the water where he fell from the mast, and always, Italy, better than any book, lying in the chestnut woods, and in the fall mist behind the Duomo going across the town to the Ospedale Maggiore, the nails in my boots on the cobbles, and in the Spring sudden showers in the mountains and the smell of the regiment like a copper coin in your mouth. So in the heat the train stopped at Dezenzano and there was Lago de Garda and those troops are the Czech Legion, and the next time it was raining, and the next time it was in the dark, and the next time you passed it riding in a truck, and the next time you were coming from somewhere else, and the next time you walked to it in the dark from Sermione. For we have been there in the books and out of the books—and where we go, if we are any good, there you can go as we have been. A country, finally, erodes and the dust blows away, the people all die and none of them were of any importance permanently, except those who practised the arts, and these now wish to cease their work because it is too lonely, too hard to do, and is not fashionable. A thousand years makes economics silly and a work of art endures forever, but it is very difficult to do and now it is not fashionable. People do not want to do it any more because they will be out of fashion and the lice who crawl on literature will not praise them. Also it is very hard to do. So what? So I would go on reading about the river that the Tartars came across when raiding, and the drunken old hunter and the girl and how it was then in the different seasons.

Pop was reading *Richard Carvell*. We had bought

what there was to buy in Nairobi and we were pretty well to the end of the books.

"I've read this before," Pop said. "But it's a good story."

"I can just remember it. But it was a good story then."

"It's a jolly good story but I wish I hadn't read it before."

"This is terrible," P. O. M. said. "You couldn't read it."

"Do you want this one?"

"Don't be ornamental," she said. "No. I'll finish this."

"Go on. Take it."

"I'll give it right back."

"Hey, M'Cola," I said. "Beer?"

"N'Dio," he said with great force, and from the chop box one of the natives had carried on his head produced, in its straw casing, a bottle of German beer, one of the sixty-four bottles Dan had bought from the German trading station. Its neck was wrapped in silver foil and on its black and yellow label there was a horseman in armor. It was still cool from the night and opened by the tin opener it creamed into three cups, thick-foamed, full-bodied.

"No," said Pop. "Very bad for the liver."

"Come on."

"All right."

We all drank and when M'Cola opened the second bottle Pop refused, firmly.

"Go on. It means more to you. I'm going to take a nap."

"Poor old Mama?"

"Just a little."

"All for me," I said. M'Cola smiled and shook his head at this drinking. I lay back against the tree and watched the wind bringing the clouds and drank the beer slowly out of the bottle. It was cooler that way and it was excellent beer. After a while Pop and P. O. M. were both asleep and I got back the Sevastopol book and read in the Cossacks again. It was a good story.

When they woke up we had lunch of cold sliced tenderloin, bread, and mustard, and a can of plums, and drank the third, and last, bottle of beer. Then we read again and all went to sleep. I woke thirsty and was unscrewing the top from a water bottle when I heard a rhino snort and crash in the brush of the river bed. Pop was awake and heard it too and we took our guns, without speaking, and started toward where the noise had come from. M'Cola found the tracks. The rhino had come up the stream, evidently he had winded us when he was only about thirty yards away, and had gone on up. We could not follow the tracks the way the wind was blowing so we circled away from the stream and back to the edge of the burned place to get above him and then hunted very carefully against the wind along the stream through very thick bush, but we did not find him. Finally Droopy found where he had gone up the other side and on into the hills. From the tracks it did not seem a particularly large one.

We were a long way from camp, at least four hours as we had come, and much of it up-hill going back, certainly there would be that long climb out of the canyon; we had a wounded buffalo to deal with, and when we came out on the edge of the burned country again, we agreed that we should get P. O. M. and get started. It was still hot, but the sun was on its way down and for a good way we would be on the heavily shaded game trail on the high bank above the stream. When we found P. O. M. she pretended to be indignant at our going off and leaving her alone but she was only teasing us.

We started off, Droop and his spearsman in the lead, walking along the shadow of the trail that was broken by the sun through the leaves. Instead of the cool early morning smell of the forest there was a nasty stink like the mess cats make.

"What makes the stink?" I whispered to Pop.

"Baboons," he said.

A whole tribe of them had gone on just ahead of us and their droppings were everywhere. We came up to the place where the rhinos and the buff had come out of the reeds and I located where I thought the buff had been when I shot. M'Cola and Droopy were casting about like hounds and I thought they were at least fifty yards too high up the bank when Droop held up a leaf.

"He's got blood," Pop said. We went up to them.

There was a great quantity of blood, black now on the grass, and the trail was easy to follow. Droop and M'Cola trailed one on each side, leaving the trail between them, pointing to each blood spot formally with a long stem of grass. I always thought it would be better for one to trail slowly and the other cast ahead but this was the way they trailed, stooped heads, pointing each dried splash with their grass stems and occasionally, when they picked up the tracks after losing them, stooping to pluck a grass blade or a leaf that had the black stain on it. I followed them with the Springfield, then came Pop, with P. O. M. behind him. Droop carried my big gun and Pop had his. M'Cola had P. O. M.'s Mannlicher slung over his shoulder. None of us spoke and every one seemed to regard it as a pretty serious business. In some high grass we found blood, at a pretty good height on the grass leaves on both sides of the trail where the buff had gone through the grass. That meant he was shot clean through. You could not tell the original color of the blood now, but I had a moment of hoping he might be shot through the lungs. But further on we came on some droppings in the rocks with blood in them and then for a while he had dropped dung wherever he climbed and all of it was blood-spotted. It looked, now, like a gut shot or one through the paunch. I was more ashamed of it all the time.

"If he comes don't worry about Droopy or the others," Pop whispered. "They'll get out of his way. Stop him."

"Right up the nose," I said.

"Don't try anything fancy," Pop said. The trail climbed steadily, then twice looped back on itself and for a time seemed to wander, without plan, among some rocks, Once it led down to the stream, crossed a rivulet of it and then came back up on the same bank, grading up through the trees.

"I think we'll find him dead," I whispered to Pop. That aimless turn had made me see him, slow and hard hit, getting ready to go down.

"I hope so," Pop said.

But the trail went on, where there was little grass now, and trailing was much slower and more difficult. There were no tracks now that I could see, only the probable line he would take, verified by a shiny dark splatter of dried blood on a stone. Several times we lost it entirely and, the three of us making casts, one would find it, point and whisper "Damu," and we would go on again. Finally it led down from a rocky hillside with the last of the sun on it, down into the stream bed where there was a long, wide patch of the highest dead reeds that we had seen. These were higher and thicker even than the slough the buff had come out of in the morning and there were several game trails that went into them.

"Not good enough to take the little Memsahib in there," Pop said.

"Let her stay here with M'Cola," I said.

"It's not good enough for the little Memsahib," Pop repeated. "I don't know why we let her come."

"She can wait here. Droop wants to go on."

"Right you are. We'll have a look."

"You wait here with M'Cola," I whispered over my shoulder.

We followed Droopy into the thick, tall grass that was five feet above our heads, walking carefully on the game trail, stooping forward, trying to make no noise breathing. I was thinking of the buff the way I had seen them when we had gotten the three that time, how the old bull had come out of the bush, groggy as he was, and I could see the horns, the boss coming far down, the muzzle out, the little eyes, the roll of fat and muscle on his thin-haired, gray, scaly-hided neck, the heavy power and the rage in him, and I admired him and respected him, but he was slow, and all the while we shot I felt that it was fixed and that we had him. This was different, this was no rapid fire, no pouring it on him as he comes groggy into the open, if he comes now I must be quiet inside and put it down his nose as he comes with the head out. He will have to put the head down to hook, like any bull, and that will uncover the old place the boys wet their knuckles on and I will get one in there and then must go sideways into the grass and he would be Pop's from then on unless I could keep the rifle when I jumped. I was sure I could get that one in and jump if I could wait and watch his head come down. I knew I could do that and that the shot would kill him but how long would it take? That was the whole thing. How long would it take? Now, going for-

ward, sure he was in here, I felt the elation, the best elation of all, of certain action to come, action in which you
had something to do, in which you can kill and come out
of it, doing something you are ignorant about and so not
scared, no one to worry about and no responsibility except to perform something you feel sure you can perform,
and I was walking softly ahead watching Droopy's back
and remembering to keep the sweat out of my glasses
when I heard a noise behind us and turned my head. It
was P. O. M. with M'Cola coming on our tracks.

"For God's sake," Pop said. He was furious.

We got her back out of the grass and up onto the bank
and made her realize that she must stay there. She had
not understood that she was to stay behind. She had
heard me whisper something but thought it was for her
to come behind M'Cola.

"That spooked me," I said to Pop.

"She's like a little terrier," he said. "But it's not good
enough."

We were looking out over that grass.

"Droop wants to go still," I said. "I'll go as far as he
will. When he says no that lets us out. After all, I gut-
shot the son of a bitch."

"Mustn't do anything silly, though."

"I can kill the son of a bitch if I get a shot at him. If
he comes he's got to give me a shot."

The fright P. O. M. had given us about herself had
made me noisy.

"Come on," said Pop. We followed Droopy back in
and it got worse and worse and I do not know about Pop
but about half way I changed to the big gun and kept the
safety off and my hand over the trigger guard and I was
plenty nervous by the time Droopy stopped and shook
his head and whispered "Hapana." It had gotten so you
could not see a foot ahead and it was all turns and twists.
It was really bad and the sun was only on the hillside
now. We both felt good because we had made Droopy
do the calling off and I was relieved as well. What we
had followed him into had made my fancy shooting plans
seem very silly and I knew all we had in there was Pop
to blast him over with the four-fifty number two after
I'd maybe miss him with that lousy four-seventy. I had
no confidence in anything but its noise any more.

We were back trailing when we heard the porters on
the hillside shout and we ran crashing through the grass
to try to get to a high enough place to see to shoot. They
waved their arms and shouted that the buffalo had come
out of the reeds and gone past them and then M'Cola and
Droopy were pointing and Pop had me by the sleeve
trying to pull me to where I could see them and then, in
the sunlight, high up on the hillside against the rocks I
saw two buffalo. They shone very black in the sun and
one was much bigger than the other and I remember
thinking this was our bull and that he had picked up a
cow and she had made the pace and kept him going.
Droop had handed me the Springfield and I slipped my

arm through the sling and sighting, the buff now all seen
through the aperture, I froze myself inside and held the
bead on the top of his shoulder and as I started to squeeze
he started running and I swung ahead of him and loosed
off. I saw him lower his head and jump like a bucking
horse as he comes out of the chutes and as I threw the
shell, slammed the bolt forward and shot again, behind
him as he went out of sight, I knew I had him. Droopy
and I started to run and as we were running I heard a low
bellow. I stopped and yelled at Pop, "Hear him? I've
got him, I tell you!"

"You hit him," said Pop. "Yes."

"Goddamn it, I killed him. Didn't you hear him bellow?"

"No."

"Listen!" We stood listening and there it came, clear,
a long, moaning, unmistakable bellow.

"By God," Pop said. It was a very sad noise.

M'Cola grabbed my hand and Droopy slapped my back
and all laughing we started on a running scramble, sweating, rushing, up the ridge through the trees and over
rocks. I had to stop for breath, my heart pounding, and
wiped the sweat off my face and cleaned my glasses.

"Kufa!" M'Cola said, making the word for dead almost explosive in its force. "N'Dio! Kufa!"

"Kufa!" Droopy said grinning.

"Kufa!" M'Cola repeated and we shook hands again
before we went on climbing. Then, ahead of us, we saw

him, on his back, throat stretched out to the full, his weight on his horns, wedged against a tree. M'Cola put his finger in the bullet hole in the center of the shoulder and shook his head happily.

Pop and P. O. M. came up, followed by the porters.

"By God, he's a better bull than we thought," I said.

"He's not the same bull. This is a real bull. That must have been our bull with him."

"I thought he was with a cow. It was so far away I couldn't tell."

"It must have been four hundred yards. By God, you *can* shoot that little pipsqueak."

"When I saw him put his head down between his legs and buck I knew we had him. The light was wonderful on him."

"I knew you had hit him, and I knew he wasn't the same bull. So I thought we had two wounded buffalo to deal with. I didn't hear the first bellow."

"It was wonderful when we heard him bellow," P. O. M. said. "It's such a sad sound. It's like hearing a horn in the woods."

"It sounded awfully jolly to me," Pop said. "By God, we deserve a drink on this. That was a shot. Why didn't you ever tell us you could shoot?"

"Go to hell."

"You know he's a damned good tracker, too, and what kind of a bird shot?" he asked P. O. M.

"Isn't he a beautiful bull?" P. O. M. asked.

"He's a fine one. He's not old but it's a fine head."

We tried to take pictures but there was only the little box camera and the shutter stuck and there was a bitter argument about the shutter while the light failed, and I was nervous now, irritable, righteous, pompous about the shutter and inclined to be abused because we could get no picture. You cannot live on a plane of the sort of elation I had felt in the reeds and having killed, even when it is only a buffalo, you feel a little quiet inside. Killing is not a feeling that you share and I took a drink of water and told P. O. M. I was sorry I was such a bastard about the camera. She said it was all right and we were all right again looking at the buff with M'Cola making the cuts for the headskin and we standing close together and feeling fond of each other and understanding everything, camera and all. I took a drink of the whiskey and it had no taste and I felt no kick from it.

"Let me have another," I said. The second one was all right.

We were going on ahead to camp with the chased-by-a-rhino spearsman as guide and Droop was going to skin out the head and they were going to butcher and cache the meat in trees so the hyenas would not get it. They were afraid to travel in the dark and I told Droopy he could keep my big gun. He said he knew how to shoot so I took out the shells and put on the safety and handing it to him told him to shoot. He put it to his shoulder, shut the wrong eye, and pulled hard on the trigger, and again, and again. Then I showed him about the safety and had him put it on and off and snap the gun a couple of times. M'Cola became very superior during Droopy's struggle to fire with the safety on and Droopy seemed to get much smaller. I left him the gun and two cartridges and they were all busy butchering in the dusk when we followed the spearsman and the tracks of the smaller buff, which had no blood on them, up to the top of the hill and on our way toward home. We climbed around the tops of valleys, went across gulches, up and down ravines and finally came onto the main ridge, it dark and cold in the evening, the moon not yet up, we plodded along, all tired. Once M'Cola, in the dark, loaded with Pop's heavy gun and an assortment of water bottles, binoculars, and a musette bag of books, sung out a stream of what sounded like curses at the guide who was striding ahead.

"What's he say?" I asked Pop.

"He's telling him not to show off his speed. That there is an old man in the party."

"Who does he mean, you or himself?"

"Both of us."

We saw the moon come up, smoky red over the brown hills, and we came down through the chinky lights of the village, the mud houses all closed tight, and the smells of goats and sheep, and then across the stream and up the bare slope to where the fire was burning in front of our tents. It was a cold night with much wind.

In the morning we hunted, picked up a track at a spring and trailed a rhino all over the high orchard country before he went down into a valley that led, steeply, into the canyon. It was very hot and the tight boots of the day before had chafed P. O. M.'s feet. She did not complain about them but I could see they hurt her. We were all luxuriantly, restfully tired.

"The hell with them," I said to Pop. "I don't want to kill another one unless he's big. We might hunt a week for a good one. Let's stand on the one we have and pull out and join Karl. We can hunt oryx down there and get those zebra hides and get on after the kudu."

We were sitting under a tree on the summit of a hill and could see off over all the country and the canyon running down to the Rift Valley and Lake Manyara.

"It would be good fun to take porters and a light outfit and hunt on ahead of them down through that valley and out to the lake," Pop said.

"That would be swell. We could send the trucks around to meet us at what's the name of the place?"

"Maji-Moto."

"Why don't we do that?" P. O. M. asked.

"We'll ask Droopy how the valley is."

Droopy didn't know but the spearsman said it was very rough and bad going where the stream came down through the rift wall. He did not think we could get the loads through. We gave it up.

"That's the sort of trip to make, though," Pop said. "Porters don't cost as much as petrol."

"Can't we make trips like that when we come back?" P. O. M. asked.

"Yes," Pop said. "But for a big rhino you want to go up on Mount Kenya. You'll get a real one there. Kudu's the prize here. You'd have to go up to Kalal to get one in Kenya. Then if we get them we'll have time to go on down in that Handeni country for sable."

"Let's get going," I said without moving.

Since a long time we had all felt good about Karl's rhino. We were glad he had it and all of that had taken on a correct perspective. Maybe he had his oryx by now. I hoped so. He was a fine fellow, Karl, and it was good he got these extra fine heads.

"How do you feel, poor old Mama?"

"I'm fine. If we *are* going I'll be just as glad to rest my feet. But I love this kind of hunting."

"Let's get back, eat, break camp, and get down there tonight."

That night we got into our old camp at M'utu-Umbo, under the big trees, not far from the road. It had been our first camp in Africa and the trees were as big, as spreading, and as green, the stream as clear and fast flowing, and the camp as fine as when we had first been there. The only difference was that now it was hotter at night, the road in was hub-deep in dust, and we had seen a lot of country. 123

CHAPTER

W<small>E</small> had come down to the Rift Valley by a sandy red road across a high plateau, then up and down through orchard-bushed hills, around a slope of forest to the top of the rift wall where we could look down and see the plain, the heavy forest below the wall, and the long, dried-up edged shine of Lake Manyara rose-colored at one end with a half million tiny dots that were flamingoes. From there the road dropped steeply along the face of the wall, down into the forest, onto the flatness of the valley, through cultivated patches of green corn, bananas, and trees I did not know the names of, walled thick with forest, past a Hindu's trading store and many huts,

SIX

over two bridges where clear, fast-flowing streams ran, through more forest, thinning now to open glades, and into a dusty turn-off that led into a deeply rutted, dust-filled track through bushes to the shade of M'utu-Umbu camp.

That night after dinner we heard the flamingoes flighting in the dark. It was like the sound the wings of ducks make as they go over before it is light, but slower, with a steady beat, and multiplied a thousand times. Pop and I were a little drunk and P. O. M. was very tired. Karl was gloomy again. We had taken the edge from his victory over rhino and now that was past anyway and he was facing possible defeat by oryx. Then, too, they had found not a leopard but a marvellous lion, a huge, black-maned lion that did not want to leave, on the rhino carcass when they had gone there the next morning and could not shoot him because he was in some sort of forest reserve.

"That's rotten," I said and I tried to feel bad about it but I was still feeling much too good to appreciate any one else's gloom and Pop and I sat, tired through to our bones, drinking whiskey and soda and talking.

The next day we hunted oryx in the dried-up dustiness of the Rift Valley and finally found a herd way off at the edge of the wooded hills on the far side above a Masai village. They were like a bunch of Masai donkeys except for the beautiful straight-slanting black horns and all the heads looked good. When you looked closely two or three were obviously better than the others and sitting on the ground I picked what I thought was the very best of the lot and as they strung out I made sure of this one. I heard the bullet smack and watched the oryx circle out away from the others, the circle quickening, and knew I had it. So I did not shoot again.

This was the one Karl had picked, too. I did not know that, but had shot, deliberately selfish, to make sure of the best this time at least, but he got another good one and they went off in a wind-lifted cloud of gray dust as they galloped. Except for the miracle of their horns there was no more excitement in shooting them than if they had been donkeys and after the truck came up and M'Cola and Charo had skinned the heads out and cut up the meat we rode home in the blowing dust, our faces gray with it, and the valley one long heat mirage.

We stayed at that camp two days. We had to get some zebra hides that we had promised friends at home and it needed time for the skinner to handle them properly. Getting the zebra was no fun; the plain was dull, now that the grass had dried, hot and dusty after the hills, and the picture that remains is of sitting against an ant hill with, in the distance, a herd of zebra galloping in the gray heat haze, raising a dust, and on the yellow plain, the birds circling over a white patch there, another beyond, there a third, and looking back, the plume of dust of the truck coming with the skinners and the men to cut up the meat for the village. I did some bad shooting in the heat on a Grant's gazelle that the volunteer skinners asked me to kill them for meat, wounding him in a running shot after missing him three or four times, and then following him across the plain until almost noon in that heat until I got within range and killed him.

But that afternoon we went out along the road that ran through the settlement and past the corner of the Hindu's general store, where he smiled at us in well-oiled, unsuccessful-storekeeping, brotherly humanity, and hopeful salesmanship, turned the car off to the left onto

a track that went into the deep forest, a narrow brush-
bordered track through the heavy timber, that crossed
a stream on an unsound log and pole bridge and went
on until the timber thinned and we came out into a grassy
savannah that stretched ahead to the reed-edged, dried-
up bed of the lake with, far beyond, the shine of the water
and the rose-pink of the flamingoes. There were some
grass huts of fishermen in the shade of the last trees
and ahead the wind blew across the grass of the savannah and the dried bed of the lake showed a white-gray
with many small animals humping across its baked surface as our car alarmed them. They were reed buck and
they looked strange and awkward as they moved in the
distance but trim and graceful as you saw them standing
close. We turned the car out through the thick, short
grass and onto the dried lake floor and everywhere, to
the left and to the right, where the streams flowed out
into the lake and made a reedy marsh that ran down
toward the receded lake, cut by canals of water, ducks
were flying and we could see big flocks of geese spread
over the grassy hummocks that rose above the marsh.
The dried bed was hard and firm and we drove the car
until it commenced to look moist and soft ahead, then
left the motor car standing there, and, Karl taking Charo
and I, M'Cola to carry shells and birds, we agreed to
work one on one side and one the other of the marsh and
try to shoot and keep the birds moving while Pop and
P. O. M. went into the edge of the high reeds on the left

shore of the lake where another stream made a thick marsh to which we thought the ducks might fly.

We saw them walk across the open, a big bulky figure in a faded corduroy coat and a very small one in trousers, gray khaki jacket, boots, and a big hat, and then disappear as they crouched in a point of dried reeds before we started. But as we went out to reach the edge of the stream we soon saw the plan was no good. Even watching carefully for the firmest footing you sunk down in the cool mud to the knees and, as it became less mucky and there were more hummocks broken by water, sometimes I went in to the waist. The ducks and geese flew up out of range and after the first flock had swung across toward where the others were hidden in the reeds and we heard the sharp, small, double report of P. O. M.'s 28-gauge and saw the ducks wheel off and go out toward the lake, the other scattered flocks and the geese all went out toward the open water. A flock of dark ibises, looking, with their dipped bills, like great curlews, flew over from the marsh on the side of the stream where Karl was and circled high above us before they went back into the reeds. All through the bog were snipe and black and white godwits and finally, not being able to get within range of the ducks, I began to shoot snipe to M'Cola's great disgust. We followed the marsh out and then I crossed another stream, shoulder high, holding my gun and shooting coat with shells in the pocket above my head and finally trying to work toward where

P. O. M. and Pop were, found a deep flowing stream where teal were flying, and killed three. It was nearly dark now and I found Pop and P. O. M. on the far bank of this stream at the edge of the dried lake bed. It all looked too deep to wade and the bottom was soft but finally I found a heavily worn hippo trail that went into the stream and treading on this, the bottom fairly firm under foot, I made it, the water coming just under my armpits. As I came out on the grass and stood dripping a flock of teal came over very fast and, crouching to shoot in the dusk at the same time Pop did, we cut down three that fell hard in a long slant ahead in the tall grass. We hunted carefully and found them all. Their speed had carried them much farther than we expected and then, almost dark now, we started for the car across the gray dried mud of the lake bed, me soaked and my boots squashing water, P. O. M. pleased with the ducks, the first we'd had since the Serengetti, we all remembering how marvellous they were to eat, and ahead we could see the car looking very small and beyond it a stretch of flat, baked mud and then the grassy savannah and the forest.

Next day we came in from the zebra business gray and sweat-caked with dust that the car raised and the wind blew over us on the way home across the plain. P. O. M. and Pop had not gone out, there was nothing for them to do and no need for them to eat that dust, and Karl and I out on the plain in the too much sun and dust had gone through one of those rows that starts like this, "What was the matter?"

"They were too far."

"Not at the start."

"They were too far, I tell you."

"They get hard if you don't take them."

"You shoot them."

"I've got enough. We only want twelve hides altogether. You go ahead."

Then some one, angry, shooting too fast to show he was being asked to shoot too fast, getting up from behind the ant hill and turning away in disgust, walking toward his partner, who says, smugly, "What's the matter with them?"

"They're too damned far, I tell you," desperately.

The smug one, complacently, "Look at them."

The zebra that had galloped off had seen the approaching truck of the skinners and had circled and were standing now, broadside, in easy range.

The one looks, says nothing, too angry now to shoot. Then says, "Go ahead. Shoot."

The smug one, more righteous now than ever, refuses. "Go ahead," he says.

"I'm through," says the other. He knows he is too angry to shoot and he feels he has been tricked. Something is always tricking him, the need to do things other than in a regular order, or by an inexact command in which details are not specified, or to have to do it in front of people, or to be hurried.

"We've got eleven," says smug face, sorry now. He knows he should not hurry him, that he should leave him alone, that he only upsets him by trying to speed him up, and that he has been a smugly righteous bastard again. "We can pick up the other one any time. Come on, Bo, we'll go in."

"No, let's get him. You get him."

"No, let's go in."

And as the car comes up and you ride in through the dust the bitterness goes and there is only the feeling of shortness of time again.

"What you thinking about now?" you ask. "What a son of a bitch I am, still?"

"About this afternoon," he says and grins, making wrinkles in the caked dust on his face.

"Me too," you say.

Finally the afternoon comes and you start.

This time you wear canvas ankle-high boots, light to pull out when you sink, you work out from hummock to hummock, picking a way across the marsh and wade and flounder through the canals and the ducks fly as before out to the lake, but you make a long circle to the right and come out into the lake itself and find the bottom hard and firm and walking knee deep in the water get outside the big flocks, then there is a shot and you and M'Cola crouch, heads bent, and then the air is full of them, and you cut down two, then two again, and then a high one straight overhead, then miss a fast one straight and low to the right, then they come whistling back, passing faster than you can load and shoot, you brown a bunch to get cripples for decoys and then take only fancy shots because you know now you can get all that we can use or carry. You try the high one, straight overhead and almost leaning backward, the *coup de roi,* and splash a big black duck down beside M'Cola, him laughing, then, the four cripples swimming away, you decide you better kill them and pick up. You have to run in water to your knees to get in range of the last cripple and you slip and go face down and are sitting, enjoying being completely wet finally, water cool on your behind, soaked with muddy water, wiping off glasses and then getting the water out of the gun, wondering if you can shoot up the shells before they will swell, M'Cola delighted with the spill. He, with the shooting coat now full of ducks, crouches and a flock of geese pass over in easy range while you try to pump a wet shell in. You get a shell in, shoot, but it is too far, or you were behind, and at the shot you see the cloud of flamingoes rise in the sun, making the whole horizon of the lake pink. Then they settle. But after that each time after you shoot you turn and look out into the sun on the water and see that quick rise of the unbelievable cloud and then the slow settling.

" 'Cola," you say and point.

"N'Dio," he says, watching them. "M'uzuri!" and hands you more shells.

We all had good shooting but it was best out on the lake and for three days afterward, travelling, we had cold teal, the best of ducks to eat, fine, plump, and tender, cold with Pan-Yan pickles, and the red wine we bought at Babati sitting by the road waiting for the trucks to come up, sitting on the shady porch of the little hotel at Babati, then late at night when the trucks finally came in and we were at the house of an absent friend of a friend, high up in the hills, cold at night, wearing coats at the table, having waited so long for the broken-down truck to come that we all drank much too much and were unspeakably hungry, P. O. M. dancing with the manager of the coffee shamba, and with Karl, to the gramophone, me shot full of emetine and with a ring-ing headache drowning it successfully in whiskey-soda with Pop on the porch, it dark and the wind blowing a gale, and then those teal coming on the table, smoking hot and with fresh vegetables. Guinea hen were all right, and I had one now in the lunch box in the back of the car that I would eat tonight; but those teal were the finest of all.

From Babati we had driven through the hills to the edge of a plain, wooded in a long stretch of glade beyond a small village where there was a mission station at the foot of a mountain. Here we had made a camp to hunt kudu which were supposed to be in the wooded hills and in the forest on the flats that stretched out to the edge of the open plain.

CHAPTER

I T was a hot place to camp, under trees that had been
girdled to kill them so that the tse-tse fly would leave,
and there was hard hunting in the hills, which were
steep, brushy, and very broken, with a hard climb before you got up into them, and easy hunting on the
wooded flats where you wandered as though through a
deer park. But everywhere were tse-tse flies, swarming
around you, biting hard on your neck, through your
shirt, on arms, and behind the ears. I carried a leafy
branch and swished away at the back of my neck as we
walked and we hunted five days, from daylight until
dark, coming home after dark, dead tired but glad of

SEVEN

the coolness and of the darkness that stopped the tse-tse from biting. We took turns hunting the hills and the flats and Karl became steadily gloomier although he killed a very fine roan antelope. He had gotten a very complicated personal feeling about kudu and, as always when he was confused, it was some one's fault, the guides, the choice of beat, the hills; these all betrayed him. The hills punished him and he did not believe in the flats. Each day I hoped he would get one and that the atmosphere would clear but each day his feelings about the kudu complicated the hunting. He was never a climber and took real punishment in the hills. I tried

137

to take the bulk of the hill beats to relieve him but I could see, now that he was tired he felt they probably *were* in the hills and he was missing his chance.

In the five days I saw a dozen or more kudu cows and one young bull with a string of cows. The cows were big, gray, striped-flanked antelope with ridiculously small heads, big ears, and a soft, fast-rushing gait that moved them in big-bellied panic through the trees. The young bull had the start of a spiral on his horns but they were short and dumpy and as he ran past us at the end of a glade in the dusk, third in a string of six cows, he was no more like a real bull than a spike elk is like a big, old, thick-necked, dark-maned, wonder-horned, tawny-hided, beer-horse-built bugler of a bull-elk.

Another time, headed home as the sun went down along a steep valley in the hills, the guides pointed to two gray, white-striped, moving animals, against the sun at the top of the hill, showing only their flanks through the trunks of the trees and said they were kudu bulls. We could not see the horns and when we got up to the top of the hill the sun was gone and on the rocky ground we could not find their tracks. But from the glimpse we had they looked higher in the legs than the cows we saw and they might have been bulls. We hunted the ridges until dark but never saw them again nor did Karl find them the next day when we sent him there.

We jumped many water buck and once, still hunting along a ridge with a steep gully below, we came on a water buck that had heard us, but not scented us, and as we stood, perfectly quiet, M'Cola holding his hand on mine, we watched him, only a dozen feet away, standing, beautiful, dark, full-necked, a dark ruff on his neck, his horns up, trembling all over as his nostrils widened searching for the scent. M'Cola was grinning, pressing his fingers tight on my wrist and we watched the big buck shiver from the danger that he could not locate. Then there was the distant, heavy boom of a native black powder gun and the buck jumped and almost ran over us as he crashed up the ridge.

Another day, with P. O. M. along, we had hunted all through the timbered flat and come out to the edge of the plain where there were only clumps of bush and san-seviera when we heard a deep, throaty, cough. I looked at M'Cola.

"Simba," he said and did not look pleased.

"Wapi?" I whispered. "Where?"

He pointed.

I whispered to P. O. M., "It's a lion. Probably the one we heard early this morning. You go back to those trees."

We had heard a lion roaring just before daylight when we were getting up.

"I'd rather stay with you."

"It wouldn't be fair to Pop," I said. "You wait back there."

"All right. But you *will* be careful."

"I won't take anything but a standing shot and I won't shoot unless I'm sure of him."

"All right."

"Come on," I said to M'Cola.

He looked very grave and did not like it at all.

"Wapi Simba?" I whispered.

"Here," he said dismally and pointed at the broken islands of thick, green spiky cover. I motioned to one of the guides to go back with P. O. M. and we watched them go back a couple of hundred yards to the edge of the forest.

"Come on," I said. M'Cola shook his head without smiling but followed. We went forward very slowly, looking into and trying to see through the senseviera. We could see nothing. Then we heard the cough again, a little ahead and to the right.

"*No!*" M'Cola whispered. "*Hapana,* B'wana!"

"Come on," I said. I pointed my forefinger into my neck and wriggled the thumb down. "Kufa," I whispered, meaning that I would shoot the bastard in the neck and kill him dead. M'Cola shook his head, his face dead grave and sweating. "Hapana!" he whispered.

There was an ant hill ahead and we climbed the furrowed clay and from the top looked all around. We could not make out anything in the green cactus-like cover. I had believed we might see him from the ant hill and after we came down we went on for about two hundred yards into the broken cactus. Once again we heard him cough ahead of us and once, a little farther on, we heard a growl. It was very deep and very impressive. Since the ant heap my heart had not been in it. Until that had failed I had believed I might have a close and good shot and I knew that if I could kill one alone, without Pop along, I would feel good about it for a long time. I had made up my mind absolutely not to shoot unless I knew I could kill him, I had killed three and knew what it consisted in, but I was getting more excitement from this one than the whole trip. I felt it was perfectly fair to Pop to take it on as long as I had a chance to call the shot but what we were getting into now was bad. He kept moving away as we came on, but slowly. Evidently he did not want to move, having fed, probably, when we had heard him roaring in the early morning, and he wanted to settle down now. M'Cola hated it. How much of it was the responsibility he felt for me to Pop and how much was his own acute feeling of misery about the dangerous game I did not know. But he felt very miserable. Finally he put his hand on my shoulder, put his face almost into mine and shook his head violently three times.

"Hapana! Hapana! Hapana! B'wana!" he protested, sorrowed, and pled.

After all, I had no business taking him where I could not call the shot and it was a profound personal relief to turn back.

"All right," I said. We turned around and came back out the same way we had gone in, then crossed the open prairie to the trees where P. O. M. was waiting.

"Did you see him?"

"No," I told her. "We heard him three or four times."

"Weren't you frightened?"

"Pea-less," I said, "at the last. But I'd rather have shot him in there than any damned thing in the world."

"My, I'm glad you're back," she said. I got the dictionary out of my pocket and made a sentence in pigeon Swahili. "Like" was the word I wanted.

"M'Cola like Simba?"

M'Cola could grin again now and the smile moved the Chinese hairs at the corner of his mouth.

"Hapana," he said, and waved his hand in front of his face. "Hapana!"

"Hapana" is a negative.

"Shoot a kudu?" I suggested.

"Good," said M'Cola feelingly in Swahili. "Better. Best. Tendalla, yes. Tendalla."

But we never saw a kudu bull out of that camp and we left two days later to go into Babati and then down to Kondoa and strike across country toward Handeni and the coast.

I never liked that camp, nor the guides, nor the country. It had that picked-over, shot-out feeling. We knew there were kudu there and the Prince of Wales had killed his kudu from that camp, but there had been three other parties in that season, and the natives were hunting, supposedly defending their crops from baboons, but on meeting a native with a brass-bound musket it seemed odd that he should follow the baboons ten miles away from his shamba up into the kudu hills to have a shot at them, and I was all for pulling out and trying the new country toward Handeni where none of us had ever been.

"Let's go then," Pop said.

It seemed this new country was a gift. Kudu came out into the open and you sat and waited for the more enormous ones and selecting a suitable head, blasted him over. Then there were sable and we agreed that whoever killed the first kudu should move on in the sable country. I was beginning to feel awfully good and Karl was very cheerful at the prospect of this new miraculous country where they were so unsophisticated that it was really a shame to topple them over.

We left, soon after daylight, ahead of the outfit, who were to strike camp and follow in the two lorries. We stopped in Babati at the little hotel overlooking the lake and bought some more Pan-Yan pickles and had some cold beer. Then we started south on the Cape to Cairo road, here well graded, smooth, and carefully cut through wooded hills overlooking the long yellow stretch of plains of the Masai Steppes, down and through farming country, where the dried-breasted old women and the shrunken-flanked, hollow-ribbed old men hoed in the cornfields, through miles and dusty miles of this, and then into a valley of sun-baked, eroded land where the soil was blowing away in clouds as you looked, into the tree-shaded, pretty, whitewashed, German model-garrison town of Kandoa-Irangi.

We left M'Cola at the crossroads to hold up our lorries when they came, put the car into some shade and visited the military cemetery. We intended to call on the D. O. but they were at lunch, and we did not want to bother them, so after the military cemetery which was a pleasant, clean, well-kept place and as good as another to be dead in, we had some beer under a tree in shade that seemed liquid cool after the white glare of a sun that you could feel the weight of on your neck and shoulders, started the car and went out to the crossroads to pick up the lorries and head to the east into the new country.

T was a wide expanse of inland sea, the surface of which
rolled away from us, like an unbroken prairie of water,
until on the far off horizon-line at the north, it was merged
and blended with the sky itself. There, all this afternoon, a
mirage, singular enough, but not so rare, and not so striking. The
country was so much lower down than the sun, it believed

CHAPTER

IT was a new country to us but it had the marks of the oldest countries. The road was a track over shelves of solid rock, worn by the feet of the caravans and the cattle, and it rose in the boulder-strewn un-roadliness through a double line of trees and into the hills. The country was so much like Aragon that I could not believe that we were not in Spain until, instead of mules with saddle bags, we met a dozen natives bare-legged and bare-headed dressed in white cotton cloth they wore gathered over the shoulder like a toga; but when they were past, the high trees beside the track over those rocks was Spain and I had followd this same route forced on ahead

EIGHT

and following close behind a horse one time watching the horror of the flies scuttling around his crupper. They were the same camel flies we found here on the lions. In Spain if one got inside your shirt you had to get the shirt off to kill him. He'd go inside the neckband, down the back, around and under one arm, make for the navel and the belly band, and if you did not get him he would move with such intelligence and speed that, scuttling flat and uncrushable he would make you undress completely to kill him.

That day of watching the camel flies working under the horse's tail, having had them myself, gave me more horror than anything I could remember except one time in a hospital with my right arm broken off short between the elbow and the shoulder, the back of the hand having hung down against my back, the points of the bone having cut up the flesh of the biceps until it finally rotted, swelled, burst, and sloughed off in pus. Alone with the pain in the night in the fifth week of not sleeping I thought suddenly how a bull elk must feel if you break a shoulder and he gets away and in that night I lay and felt it all, the whole thing as it would happen from the shock of the bullet to the end of the business and, being a little out of my head, thought perhaps what I was going through was a punishment for all hunters. Then, getting well, decided if it was a punishment I had paid it and at least I knew what I was doing. I did nothing that had not been done to me. I had been shot and I had been crippled and gotten away. I expected, always, to be killed by one thing or another and I, truly, did not mind that any more. Since I still loved to hunt I resolved that I would only shoot as long as I could kill cleanly and as soon as I lost that ability I would stop.

If you serve time for society, democracy, and the other things quite young, and declining any further enlistment make yourself responsible only to yourself, you exchange the pleasant, comforting stench of comrades for something you can never feel in any other way than by yourself. That something I cannot yet define completely but the feeling comes when you write well and truly of something and know impersonally you have written in that way and those who are paid to read it and report on it do not like the subject so they say it is all a fake, yet you know its value absolutely; or when you do something which people do not consider a serious occupation and yet you know, truly, that it is as important and has always been as important as all the things that are in fashion, and when, on the sea, you are alone with it and know that this Gulf Stream you are living with, knowing, learning about, and loving, has moved, as it moves, since before man, and that it has gone by the shoreline of that long, beautiful, unhappy island since before Columbus sighted it and that the things you find out about it, and those that have always lived in it are permanent and of value because that stream will flow, as it has flowed, after the Indians, after the Spaniards, after the British, after the Americans and after all the Cubans and all the systems of governments, the richness, the poverty, the martyrdom, the sacrifice and the venality and the cruelty are all gone as the high-piled scow of garbage, bright-colored, white-flecked, ill-smelling, now tilted on its side, spills off its load into the blue water, turning it a pale green to a depth of four or five fathoms as the load spreads across the surface, the sinkable part going down and the flotsam of palm fronds, corks, bottles, and used electric light globes, seasoned with an occasional condom or a deep floating corset, the torn leaves of a student's exercise book, a well-inflated dog, the occasional rat, the no-longer-distinguished cat; all this well shepherded by the boats of the garbage pickers who pluck their prizes with long poles, as interested, as intelligent, and as accurate as historians; they have the viewpoint; the stream, with no visible flow, takes five loads of this a day when things are going well in La Habana and in ten miles along the coast it is as clear and blue and unimpressed as it was ever before the tug hauled out the scow; and the palm fronds of our victories, the worn light bulbs of our discoveries and the empty condoms of our great loves float with no significance against one single, lasting thing—the stream.

So, in the front seat, thinking of the sea and of the country, in a little while we ran out of Aragon and down to the bank of a sand river, half a mile wide, of golden-colored sand, shored by green trees and broken by islands of timber and in this river the water is underneath the sand and the game comes down at night and digs in the sand with sharp-pointed hoofs and water flows in and they drink. We crossed this river and by now it was getting to be afternoon and we passed many people on the road who were leaving the country ahead where there was a famine and there were small trees and close brush now beside the road and then it commenced to climb and we came into some blue hills, old, worn, wooded hills with trees like beeches and clusters of huts with fire smoking and cattle home driven, flocks of sheep and goats and patches of corn and I said to P. O. M. "It's like Galicia."

"Exactly," she said. "We've been through three prov-
inces of Spain today."

"Is it really?" Pop asked.

"There's no bloody difference," I said. "Only the
buildings. It was like Navarre in Droopy's country too.
The limestone outcropping in the same way, the way the
land lies, the trees along the watercourses and the
springs."

"It's damned strange how you can love a country," Pop
said.

"You two are very profound fellows," P. O. M. said.
"But where are we going to camp?"

"Here," said Pop. "As well as any place. We'll just
find some water."

We camped under some trees near three big wells
where native women came for water and, after drawing
lots for location, Karl and I hunted in the dusk around
two of the hills across the road above the native village.

"It's all kudu country," Pop said. "You're liable to
jump one anywhere."

But we saw nothing but some Masai cattle in the timber and came home, in the dark, glad of the walk after a
day in the car, to find camp up, Pop and P. O. M. in
pyjamas by the fire, and Karl not yet in.

He came in, furious for some reason, no kudu possibly,
pale, and gaunt looking and speaking to nobody.

Later, at the fire, he asked me where we had gone

and I said we had hunted around our hill until our guide had heard them; then cut up to the top of the hill, down, and across country to camp.

"What do you mean, heard us?"

"He said he heard you. So did M'Cola."

"I thought we drew lots for where we would hunt."

"We did," I said. "But we didn't know we had gotten around to your side until we heard you."

"Did *you* hear us?"

"I heard something," I said. "And when I put my hand up to my ear to listen the guide said something to M'Cola and M'Cola said, 'B'wana.' I said, 'What B'wana?' and he said, 'B'wana Kabor.' That's you. So we figured we'd come to our limit and went up to the top and came back."

He said nothing and looked very angry.

"Don't get sore about it," I said.

"I'm not sore. I'm tired," he said. I could believe it because of all people no one can be gentler, more under-standing, more self-sacrificing, than Karl, but the kudu had become an obsession to him and he was not himself, nor anything like himself.

"He better get one pretty quick," P. O. M. said when he had gone in to his tent to bathe.

"Did you cut in on his country?" Pop asked me.

"Hell, no," I said.

"He'll get one where we're going," Pop said. "He'll probably get a fifty-incher."

"All the better," I said. "But by God, I want to get one too."

"You will, Old Timer," Pop said. "I haven't a thought but what you will."

"What the hell. We've got ten days."

"We'll get sable too, you'll see. Once our luck starts to run."

"How long have you ever had them hunt them in a good country?"

"Three weeks and leave without seeing one. And I've had them get them the first half day. It's still hunting, the way you hunt a big buck at home."

"I love it," I said. "But I don't want that guy to beat me. Pop, he's got the best buff, the best rhino, the best water-buck——"

"You beat him on oryx," Pop said.

"What's an oryx?"

"He'll look damned handsome when you get him home."

"I'm just kidding."

"You beat him on impalla, on eland. You've got a first-rate bushbuck. Your leopard's as good as his. But he'll beat you on anything where there's luck. He's got damned wonderful luck and he's a good lad. I think he's off his feed a little."

"You know how fond I am of him. I like him as well as I like any one. But I want to see him have a good time. It's no fun to hunt if we get that way about it."

"You'll see. He'll get a kudu at this next camp and he'll be on top of the wave."

"I'm just a crabby bastard," I said.

"Of course you are," said Pop. "But why not have a drink?"

"Right," I said.

Karl came out, quiet, friendly, gentle, and understandingly delicate.

"It will be fine when we get to that new country," he said.

"It will be swell," I said.

"Tell me what it's like, Mr. Phillips," he said to Pop.

"I don't know," said Pop. "But they say it's very pleasant hunting. They're supposed to feed right out in the open. That old Dutchman claims there are some remarkable heads."

"I hope you get a sixty-incher, kid," Karl said to me. "You'll get a sixty-incher."

"No," said Karl. "Don't kid me. I'll be happy with any kudu."

"You'll probably get a hell of a one," Pop said.

"Don't kid me," Karl said. "I know how lucky I've been. I would be happy with any kudu. Any bull at all."

He was very gentle and he could tell what was in your mind, forgive you for it, and understand it.

"Good old Karl," I said, warmed with whiskey, understanding, and sentiment.

"We're having a swell time, aren't we?" Karl said. "Where's poor old Mama?"

"I'm here," said P. O. M. from the shadow. "I'm one of those quiet people."

"By God if you're not," Pop said. "But you can puncture the old man quick enough when he gets started."

"That's what makes a woman a universal favorite," P. O. M. told him. "Give me another compliment, Mr. J."

"By God, you're brave as a little terrier," Pop and I had both been drinking, it seemed.

"That's lovely," P. O. M. sat far back in ·her chair, holding her hands clasped around her mosquito boots. I looked at her, seeing her quilted blue robe in the firelight now, and the light on her black hair. "I love it when you all reach the little terrier stage. Then I know the war can't be far away. Were either of you gentleman in the war by any chance?"

"Were we not," said Pop. "A couple of the bravest bastards that ever lived and your husband's an extraordinary wing shot and an excellent tracker."

"Now he's drunk, we get the truth," I said.

"Let's eat," said P. O. M. "I'm really frightfully hungry."

We were out in the car at daylight, out onto the road and beyond the village and, passing through a stretch of heavy bush, we came to the edge of a plain, still misty before the sunrise, where we could see, a long way off, eland feeding, looking huge and gray in the early morning light. We stopped the car at the edge of the bush and getting out and sitting down with the glasses saw there was a herd of kongoni scattered between us and the eland and with the kongoni a single bull oryx, like a fat, plum-colored, Masai donkey with marvellous long, black, straight, back-slanting horns that showed each time he lifted his head from feeding.

"You want to go after him?" I asked Karl.

"No. You go on."

I knew he hated to make a stalk and to shoot in front of people and so I said, "All right." Also I wanted to shoot, selfishly, and Karl was unselfish. We wanted meat badly.

I walked along the road, not looking toward the game, trying to look casual, holding the rifle slung straight up and down from the left shoulder away from the game. They seemed to pay no attention but fed away steadily. I knew that if I moved toward them they would at once move off out of range so, when from the tail of my eye I saw the oryx drop his head to feed again, and, the shot looking possible, I sat down, slipped my arm through the sling and as he looked up and started to move off, quartering away, I held for the top of his back and squeezed off. You do not hear the noise of the shot on game but the slap of the bullet sounded as he started running across and to the right, the whole plain back-grounding into moving animals against the rise of the sun, the rocking-horse canter of the long-legged, grotesque kongoni, the heavy swinging trot into gallop of the eland, and another oryx I had not seen before running with the kongoni. This sudden life and panic all made background for the one I wanted, now trotting, three-quartering away, his horns held high now and I stood to shoot running, got on him, the whole animal miniatured in the aperture and I held above his shoulders, swung ahead and squeezed and he was down, kicking, before the crack of the bullet striking bone came back. It was a very long and even more lucky shot that broke a hind leg.

I ran toward him, then slowed to walk up carefully, in order not to be blown if he jumped and ran; but he was down for good. He had gone down so suddenly and the bullet had made such a crack as it landed that I was afraid I had hit him on the horns but when I reached him he was dead from the first shot behind the shoulders high up in the back and I saw it was cutting the leg from under him that brought him down. They all came up and Charo stuck him to make him legal meat.

"Where did you hold on him the second time?" Karl asked.

"Nowhere. A touch above and quite a way ahead and swung with him."

"It was very pretty," Dan said.

"By evening," Pop said, "he'll tell us that he broke that off leg on purpose. That's one of his favorite shots, you know. Did you ever hear him explain it?"

While M'Cola was skinning the head out and Charo was

butchering out the meat, a long, thin Masai with a spear came up, said good morning, and stood, on one leg, watching the skinning. He spoke to me at some length and I called to Pop. The Masai repeated it to Pop.

"He wants to know if you are going to shoot something else," Pop said. "He would like some hides but he doesn't care about oryx hide. It is almost worthless, he says. He wonders if you would like to shoot a couple of kongoni or an eland. He likes those hides."

"Tell him on our way back."

Pop told him solemnly. The Masai shook my hand.

"Tell him he can always find me around Harry's New York Bar," I said.

The Masai said something else and scratched one leg with the other.

"He says why did you shoot him twice?" Pop asked.

"Tell him in the morning in our tribe we always shoot them twice. Later in the day we shoot them once. In the evening we are often half shot ourselves. Tell him he can always find me at the New Stanley or at Torr's."

"He says what do you do with the horns?"

"Tell him in our tribe we give the horns to our wealthiest friends. Tell him it is very exciting and sometimes members of the tribe are chased across vast spaces with empty pistols. Tell him he can find me in the book."

Pop told the Masai something and we shook hands again, parting on a most excellent basis. Looking across the plain through the mist we could see some other Masai coming along the road; earth-brown skins, and knee-ing forward stride and spears thin in the morning light.

Back in the car, the oryx head wrapped in a burlap sack, the meat tied inside the mudguards, the blood dry-ing, the meat dusting over, the road of red sand now, the plain gone, the bush again close to the edge of the road, we came up into some hills and through the little village of Kibaya where there was a white rest house and a gen-eral store and much farming land. It was here Dan had sat on a haystack one time waiting for a kudu to feed out into the edge of a patch of mealy-corn and a lion had stalked Dan while he sat and nearly gotten him. This gave us a strong historical feeling for the village of Ki-baya and as it was still cool and the sun had not yet burned off the dew from the grass I suggested we drink a bottle of that silver-paper-necked, yellow-and-black-labelled German beer with the horseman in armor on it in order that we might remember the place better and even appreciate it more. This done, full of historical admi-ration for Kibaya, we learned the road was possible ahead, left word for the lorries to follow on to the east-ward and headed on toward the coast and the kudu country.

For a long time, while the sun rose and the day became hot we drove through what Pop had described, when I asked him what the country was like to the south, as a million miles of bloody Africa, bush close to the road that was impenetrable, solid, scrubby-looking undergrowth.

"There are very big elephant in there," Pop said. "But it's impossible to hunt them. That's why they're very big. Simple, isn't it?"

After a long stretch of the million-mile country, the country began to open out into dry, sandy, bush-bordered prairies that dried into a typical desert country with occasional patches of bush where there was water, that Pop said was like the northern frontier province of Kenya. We watched for gerenuk, that long-necked antelope that resembles a praying mantis in its way of carrying itself, and for the lesser kudu that we knew lived in this desert bush, but the sun was high now and we saw nothing. Finally the road began to lift gradually into the hills again, low, blue, wooded hills now, with miles of sparse bush, a little thicker than orchard bush, between, and ahead a pair of high, heavy, timbered hills that were big enough to be mountains. These were on each side of the road and as we climbed in the car where the red road narrowed there was a herd of hundreds of cattle ahead being driven down to the coast by Somali cattle buyers, the principal buyer walked ahead, tall, good-looking in white turban and coast clothing, carrying an umbrella as a symbol of authority. We worked the car through the herd, finally, and coming out wound our way through pleasant looking bush, up and out into the open between the two mountains and on, a half a mile, to a mud and thatched village in the open clearing on a little low plateau beyond the two mountains. Looking back, the moun-

tains looked very fine with timber up their slopes, outcroppings of limestone and open glades and meadows
above the timber.

"Is this the place?"

"Yes," said Dan. "We will find where the camping
place is."

A very old, worn, and faded black man, with a stubble
of white beard, a farmer, dressed in a dirty once-white
cloth gathered at the shoulder in the manner of a Roman
toga, came out from behind one of the mud and wattle
huts, and guided us back down the road and off it to the
left to a very good camp site. He was a very discouraged-
looking old man and after Pop and Dan had talked with
him he went off, seeming more discouraged than before,
to bring some guides whose names Dan had written on a
piece of paper as being recommended by a Dutch hunter
who had been here a year ago and who was Dan's great
friend.

We took the seats out of the car to use as a table and
benches and spreading our coats to sit on had a lunch in
the deep shade of a big tree, drank some beer, and slept
or read while we waited for the lorries to come up. Before the lorries arrived the old man came back with the
skinniest, hungriest, most unsuccessful looking of Wan-
derobos who stood on one leg, scratched the back of his
neck and carried a bow and quiver of arrows and a
spear. Queried as to whether this was the guide whose
name we had the old man admitted he was not and went

off, more discouraged than ever, to get the official guides.

When we woke next the old man was standing with the two official and highly clothed in khaki guides and two others, quite naked, from the village. There was a long palaver and the head one of the two khaki-panted guides showed his credentials a To Whom It May Concern stating the bearer knew the country well and was a reliable boy and capable tracker. This was signed by so and so, professional hunter. The khaki-clothed guide referred to this professional hunter as B'wana Simba and the name infuriated us all.

"Some bloke that killed a lion once," Pop said.

"Tell him I am B'wana Fisi, the hyena slaughterer," I told Dan. "B'wana Fisi chokes them with his naked hands."

Dan was telling them something else.

"Ask them if they would like to meet B'wana Hop-Toad, the inventor of the hoptoads and Mama Tziggi, who owns all these locusts."

Dan ignored this. It seemed they were discussing money. After ascertaining their customary daily wage, Pop told them if either of us killed a kudu the guide would receive fifteen shillings.

"You mean a pound," said the leading guide.

"They seem to know what they're up to," Pop said. "I must say I don't care for this sportsman in spite of what B'wana Simba says."

B'wana Simba, by the way, we later found out to be

an excellent hunter with a wonderful reputation on the coast.

"We'll put them into two lots and you draw from them," Pop suggested, "one naked one and one with breeches in each lot. I'm all for the naked savage, myself, as a guide."

On suggesting to the two testimonial-equipped, breeched guides that they select an unclothed partner, we found this would not work out. Loud Mouth, the financial and, now, theatrical, genius who was giving a gesture-by-gesture reproduction of How B'wana Simba Killed His Last Kudu interrupted it long enough to state he would only hunt with Abdullah. Abdullah, the short, thick-nosed, educated one, was His Tracker. They always hunted together. He himself did not track. He resumed the pantomime of B'wana Simba and another character known as B'wana Doktor and the horned beasts.

"We'll take the two savages as one lot and these two Oxonians as the other," Pop said.

"I *hate* that theatrical bastard," I said.

"He may be marvellous," Pop said doubtfully. "Anyway, you're a tracker, you know. The old man says the other two are good."

"Thank you. Go to hell. Will you hold the straws?"

Pop arranged two grass stems in his fist. "The long one is for David Garrick and his pal," he explained. "The short one is the two nudist sportsmen."

"Do you want to draw first?"

"Go ahead," Karl said.

I drew David Garrick and Abdullah.

"I got the bloody tragedian."

"He may be very good," Karl said.

"Do you want to trade?"

"No. He may be a marvel."

"Now we'll draw for choice of beats. The long straw gets first choice," Pop explained.

"Go ahead and draw."

Karl drew the short one.

"What are the beats?" I asked Pop.

There was a long conversation in which our David simulated the killing of half a dozen kudu from different types of ambush, surprise, stalks in the open, and jumping them in the bush.

Finally Pop said, "It seems there's some sort of a salt lick where they come to lick salt and thousands are slain. Then sometimes you just stroll around the hill there and pot the poor buggars in the open. If you're feeling frightfully fit, you climb for them and up in the crags you knock them over as they stroll out to feed."

"I'll take the salt lick."

"Mind you only shoot the very biggest sort," Pop said.

"When do we start?" Karl asked.

"The salt lick is supposed to be an early morning show," Pop told us. "But Old Hem might as well have a look at it tonight. It's about five miles down the road before you start to walk. He'll start first and take the car. You can start back in the hills any time after the sun gets a little farther down."

"What about the Memsahib?" I asked.. "Should she go with me?"

"I don't think it's advisable," Pop said seriously. "The fewer people when you're after kudu the better."

M'Cola, Theatre Business, Abdullah, and I came back that evening late in the cool of the night and full of excitement as we came up to the fire. The dust of the salt lick had been cut up and printed deep with fresh kudu tracks and there were several big bull tracks. The blind made a marvellous ambush and I was as confident and as sure of a shot at kudu the next morning as I would be sure of a shot at ducks from a good blind, with a fine stock of decoys out, cold weather, and the certainty of a flight on.

"It's airtight. It's foolproof. It's even a shame. What's his name, Booth, Barrett, McCullough—you know who I mean——"

"Charles Laughton," said Pop, pulling on his pipe.

"That's the one. Fred Astaire. Society's hoofer and the world's. He's an ace. Found the blind and everything. Knew where the salt lick was. Could tell which way the wind blew by simply scattering dust. He's a marvel. B'wana Simba trains 'em, pal. Pop, we have them in the container. It's only a question of not spoiling the meat and selecting the more rugged specimens. I'll kill you two tomorrow on that lick. Citizens, I feel very well."

165

"What *have* you been drinking?"

"Not a damned thing, really. Call Garrick. Tell him I'll put him in the cinema. Got a part for him. Little thing I thought up on the way home. It may not work out but I like the plot. Othello or The Moor of Venice. D'you like it? It's got a wonderful idea. You see this jig we call Othello falls in love with this girl who's never been around at all so we call her Desdemona. Like it? They've been after me to write it for years but I drew the color line. Let him go out and get a reputation, I told them. Harry Wills, hell. Paulino beat him. Sharkey beat him. Dempsey beat Sharkey. Carnera knocked him out. What if nobody saw the punch? Where the hell were we, Pop? Harry Greb is dead you know."

"We were just coming into Town," Pop said. "Chaps were throwing things at you and we couldn't find out why."

"I remember," P. O. M. said. "Why didn't you make him draw the color line, Mr. J. P.?"

"I was frightfully tired," Pop said.

"You're very distinguished looking, though," P. O. M. said. "What are we going to do with this goofy?"

"Throw a drink into the brute and see if he'll quiet down."

"I'm quiet now," I said. "But by God I feel awfully good about tomorrow."

Just then who should come into camp but old Karl with his two naked savages and his half-size, very devout

166

Mohammedan gun bearer, Charo. In the firelight old Karl looked a grayish, yellowish white in the face and he took off his Stetson.

"Well, did you get one?" he asked.

"No. But they're there. What did you do?"

"Walked along a god-damned road. How do they expect to find kudu along a road with nothing but cattle and huts and people?"

He did not look like himself and I thought he must be ill. But coming in like a death's head when we had been clowning made me behave badly again and I said, "We drew lots, you know."

"Of course," he said bitterly. "We hunted along a road. What would you expect to see? Does that seem the way to hunt kudu to you?"

"But you'll get one on the salt lick in the morning," P. O. M. told him very cheerfully.

I drank off the glass of whiskey and soda and heard my voice say very cheerfully, "You'll be sure to get one on the salt lick in the morning."

"You're hunting it in the morning," Karl said.

"No. You're hunting it. I had it tonight. We're changing off. That's been understood. Isn't it, Pop?"

"Quite," Pop said. No one was looking at any one else.

"Have a whiskey and soda, Karl," P. O. M. said.

"All right," Karl said.

We had one of those quiet meals. In bed in the tent, I

said, "What in God's name prompted you to say that about him having the lick in the morning?"

"I don't know. I don't think that's what I meant to say. I got mixed up. Let's not talk about it."

"I won the damned thing drawing lots. You can't go against lots. That's the only way the luck has a chance to even up, ever."

"Don't let's talk about it."

"I don't think he's well now and he doesn't feel himself. The damned things have gotten his goat and he's liable to blow that salt lick higher than a kite in the state he's in."

"Please stop talking about it."

"I will."

"Good."

"Well, we made him feel good anyway."

"I don't know that we did. Please stop talking about it."

"I will."

"Good."

"Good night," she said.

"The hell with it," I said. "Good night."

"Good night."

...with which I had met the rough weather, the
only comparison, probably, which could avail to
the rest of my life.... It was ... at perhaps so
mild a voyage, no running, a new... great
opportunities had fluttered the circum... to use
... with sea and tempest the innocent ... with the
burning sea ... consideration and ... had attended and
that there ... tell the ... by the ... expense the
and when ... be set ... not ... the ... from the
see ... all rising as ... to ... of the ... a tiny
... of nature ... the ... in the ... by ... the
called me and I felt as ... my weight ... arise, and
placed the distance ... was the part ... west to those who
and I been a ... and ... with the ... for ... be around

179

CHAPTER

In the morning Karl and his outfit started for the salt-lick and Garrick, Abdullah, M'Cola and I crossed the road, angled behind the village up a dry watercourse and started climbing the mountains in a mist. We headed up a pebbly, boulder-filled, dry stream bed overgrown with vines and brush so that, climbing, you walked, stooping, in a steep tunnel of vines and foliage. I sweated so that I was soaked through my shirt and undergarments and when we came out on the shoulder of the mountain and stood, looking down at the bank of clouds quilting over the entire valley below us, the morning breeze chilled me and I had to put on my raincoat while we glassed the country. I was too wet with sweat to sit down and I signed Garrick to keep on going. We went around

NINE

one side of the mountain, doubled back on a higher grade
and crossed over, out of the sun that was drying my wet
shirt and along the top of a series of grassy valleys,
stopping to search each one thoroughly with the field
glasses. Finally we came to a sort of amphitheatre, a
bowl like valley of very green grass with a small stream
down the middle and timber along the far side and all the
lower edge. We sat in the shadow against some rocks,
out of any breeze, watching with the glasses as the sun
rose and lighted the opposite slopes, seeing two kudu cows
and a calf feed out from the timber, moving with the
quickly browsing, then head lifted, long staring vigilance
of all browsing animals in a forest. Animals on a plain
can see so far that they have confidence and feed very

differently from animals in the woods. We could see the vertical white stripes on their gray flanks and it was very satisfying to watch them and to be high in the mountain that early in the morning. Then, while we watched, there was a boom, like a rockslide. I thought at first it was a boulder falling, but M'Cola whispered.

"B'wana Kibor! Piga!" We listened for another shot but we did not hear one and I was sure Karl had his kudu. The cows we were watching had heard the shot and stood, listening, then went on feeding. But they fed into the timber. I remembered the old saying of the Indian in camp, "One shot, meat. Two shots, maybe. Three shots, heap shit," and I got out the dictionary to translate it for M'Cola. However it came out seemed to amuse him and he laughed and shook his head. We glassed that valley until the sun came onto us, then hunted around the other side of the mountain and in another fine valley saw the place where the other B'wana, B'wana Doktor he still sounded like, had shot a fine bull kudu, but a Masai walked down the center of the valley while we were glassing it and when I pretended I was going to shoot him Garrick became very dramatic insisting it was a man, a man, a man!

"Don't shoot men?" I asked him.

"No! No! No!" he said putting his hand to his head. I took the gun down with great reluctance, clowning for M'Cola who was grinning and, it very hot now, we walked across a meadow where the grass was knee high and truly swarming with long, rose-colored, gauzewinged locusts that rose in clouds about us, making a whirring like a mowing machine and, climbing small hills and going down a long steep slope, we made our way back to camp to find the air of the valley drifting with flying locusts and Karl already in camp with his kudu.

Passing the skinner's tent he showed me the head which looked, body-less and neck-less, the cape of hide hanging loose, wet and heavy from where the base of the skull had been severed from the vertebral column, a very strange and unfortunate kudu. Only the skin running from the eyes down to the nostrils, smooth gray and delicately marked with white, and the big, graceful ears were beautiful. The eyes were already dusty and there were flies around them and the horns were heavy, coarse, and instead of spiralling high they made a heavy turn and slanted straight out. It was a freak head, heavy and ugly.

Pop was sitting under the dining tent smoking and reading.

"Where's Karl?" I asked him.

"In his tent, I think. What did you do?"

"Worked around the hill. Saw a couple of cows."

"I'm awfully glad you got him," I told Karl at the mouth of his tent. "How was it?"

"We were in the blind and they motioned me to keep my head down and then when I looked up there he was right beside us. He looked huge."

"We heard you shoot. Where did you hit him?"

"In the leg first, I think. Then we trailed him and

finally I hit him a couple of more times and we got him."

"I heard only one shot."

"There were three or four," Karl said.

"I guess the mountain shut off some if you were gone the other way trailing him. He's got a heavy beam and a big spread."

"Thanks," Karl said. "I hope you get a lot better one. They said there was another one but I didn't see him."

I went back to the dining tent where Pop and P. O. M. were. They did not seem very elated about the kudu.

"What's the matter with you?" I asked.

"Did you see the head?" P. O. M. asked.

"Sure."

"It's *awful* looking," she said.

"It's a kudu. He's got another one still to go."

"Charo and the trackers said there was another bull with this one. A big bull with a wonderful head."

"That's all right. I'll shoot him."

"If he ever comes back."

"It's fine he has one," P. O. M. said.

"I'll bet he'll get the biggest one ever known, now," I said.

"I'm sending him down with Dan to the sable country," Pop said. "That was the agreement. The first to kill a kudu to get first crack at the sable."

"That's fine."

"Then as soon as you get your kudu we'll move down there too."

"*Good.*"

GREEN HILLS OF AFRICA

PART III

Pursuit and Failure

CHAPTER

T HAT all seemed a year ago. Now, this afternoon in the car, on the way out to the twenty-eight-mile salt-lick, the sun on our faces, just having shot the guinea fowl, having, in the last five days, failed on the lick where Karl shot his bull, having failed in the hills, the big hills and the small hills, having failed on the flats, losing a shot the night before on this lick because of the Austrian's truck, I knew there were only two days more to hunt before we must leave. M'Cola knew it too, and we were hunting together now, with no feeling of superiority on either side any more, only a shortness of time and our disgust that we did not know the country and were saddled with these farcical bastards as guides.

TEN

Kamau, the driver, was a Kikuyu, a quiet man of about thirty-five who, with an old brown tweed coat some shooter had discarded, trousers heavily patched on the knees and ripped open again, and a very ragged shirt, managed always to give an impression of great elegance. Kamau was very modest, quiet, and an excellent driver and now, as we came out of the bush country, and into an open, scrubby, desert-looking stretch, I looked at him, whose elegance, achieved with an old coat and a safety pin, whose modesty, pleasantness and skill I admired so much now, and thought how, when we first were out, he had very nearly died of fever, and that if he had died it would have meant nothing to me except that we would be short a driver; while now whenever or wherever he should die I would feel badly. Then abandoning the sweet sentiment of the distant and improbable death of Kamau, I thought what a pleasure it would be to shoot David Garrick in the behind, just to see the look on his face, sometime when he was dramatizing a stalk and, just then, we put up another flock of guineas. M'Cola handed me the shotgun and I shook my head. He nodded violently and said, "Good. Very good," and I told Kamau to go on. This confused Garrick who began an oration. Didn't we want guineas? Those were guineas. The finest kind. I had seen by the speedometer that we were only about three miles from the salt and had no desire to spook a bull off of it, by a shot, to frighten him in the way we had seen the lesser kudu leave the salt when he heard the truck noise while we were in the blind.

We left the truck under some scrubby trees about two miles from the lick and walked along the sandy road toward the first salt place which was in the open to the left of the trail. We had gone about a mile keeping absolutely quiet and walking in single file, Abdullah the educated tracker leading, then me, M'Cola, and Garrick, when we saw the road was wet ahead of us. Where the sand was thin over the clay there was a pool of water and you could see that a heavy rain had drenched it all on ahead. I did not realize what this meant but Garrick threw his arms wide, looked up to the sky and bared his teeth in anger.

"It's no good," M'Cola whispered.

Garrick started to talk in a loud voice.

"Shut up, you bastard," I said, and put my hand to my mouth. He kept on talking in above normal tones and I looked up "shut up" in the dictionary while he pointed to the sky and the rained-out road. I couldn't find "shut up" so I put the back of my hand against his mouth with some firmness and he closed it in surprise.

" 'Cola," I said.

"Yes," said M'Cola.

"What's the matter?"

"Salt no good."

"Ah."

So that was it. I had thought of the rain only as something that made tracking easy.

"When the rain?" I asked.

"Last night," M'Cola said.

Garrick started to talk and I placed the back of my hand against his mouth.

" 'Cola."

"Yes."

"Other salt," pointing in the direction of the big lick in the woods, which I knew was a good bit higher because we went very slightly up-hill through the brush to reach it. "Other salt good?"

"Maybe."

M'Cola said something in a very low voice to Garrick who seemed deeply hurt but kept his mouth shut and we went on down the road, walking around the wet places, to where, sure enough, the deep depression of the salt lick was half filled with water. Garrick started to whisper a speech here but M'Cola shut him up again.

"Come on," I said, and, M'Cola ahead, we started trailing up the damp, sandy, ordinarily dry watercourse that led through the trees to the upper lick.

M'Cola stopped dead, leaned over to look at the damp sand, then whispered, "Man," to me. There was the track.

"Shenzi," he said, which meant a wild man.

We trailed the man, moving slowly through the trees and stalking the lick carefully, up and into the blind. M'Cola shook his head.

"No good," he said. "Come on."

We went over to the lick. There it was all written plainly. There were the tracks of three big bull kudu in the moist bank beyond the lick where they had come to the salt. Then there were the sudden, deep, knifely-cut tracks where they made a spring when the bow twanged and the slashing heavily cut prints of their hoofs as they had gone off up the bank and then, far-spaced, the tracks running into the bush. We trailed them, all three, but no man's track joined theirs. The bow-man missed them.

M'Cola said, "Shenzi!" putting great hate into the word. We picked up the shenzi's tracks and saw where he had gone on back to the road. We settled down in the blind and waited there until it was dark and a light rain began to fall. Nothing came to the salt. In the rain we made our way back to the truck. Some wild-man had shot at our kudu and spooked them away from the salt and now the lick was being ruined.

Kamau had rigged a tent out of a big canvas ground cloth, hung my mosquito net inside, and set up the canvas cot. M'Cola brought the food inside the shelter tent.

Garrick and Abdullah built a fire and they, Kamau and M'Cola cooked over it. They were going to sleep in the truck. It rained drizzlingly and I undressed, got into mosquito boots and heavy pyjamas and sat on the cot, ate a breast of roast guinea hen and drank a couple of tin cups of half whiskey and water.

M'Cola came in, grave, solicitous, and very awkward inside of a tent and took my clothes out from where I had folded them to make a pillow and folded them again, very un-neatly, and put them under the blankets. He brought three tins to see if I did not want them opened.

"No."

"Chai?" he asked.

"The hell with it."

"No chai?"

"Whiskey better."

"Yes," he said feelingly. "Yes."

"Chai in the morning. Before the sun."

"Yes, B'wana M'Kumba."

"You sleep here. Out of the rain," I pointed to the

canvas where the rain was making the finest sound that we, who live much outside of houses, ever hear. It was a lovely sound, even though it was bitching us.

"Yes."

"Go on. Eat."

"Yes. No chai?"

"The hell with tea."

"Whiskey?" he asked hopefully.

"Whiskey finish."

"Whiskey," he said confidently.

"All right," I said. "Go eat," and pouring the cup half and half with water got in under the mosquito bar, found my clothes and again made them into a pillow, and lying on my side drank the whiskey very slowly, resting on one elbow, then dropped the cup down under the bar onto the ground, felt under the cot for the Springfield, put the searchlight beside me in the bed under the blanket, and went to sleep listening to the rain. I woke when I heard M'Cola come in, make his bed and go to sleep, and I woke once in the night and heard him sleeping by me; but in the morning he was up and had made the tea before I was awake.

"Chai," he said, pulling on my blanket.

"Bloody chai," I said, sitting up still asleep.

It was a gray, wet morning. The rain had stopped but the mist hung over the ground and we found the salt lick rained out and not a track near it. Then we hunted through the wet scrub on the flat hoping to find a track in the soaked earth and trail a bull until we could see him. There were no tracks. We crossed the road and followed the edge of the scrub around a moor-like open stretch. I hoped we might find the rhino but while we came on much fresh rhino dung there were no tracks since the rain. Once we heard tick birds and looking up saw them in jerky flight above us headed to the northward over the heavy scrub. We made a long circle through there but found nothing but a fresh hyena track and a cow kudu track. In a tree M'Cola pointed out a lesser kudu skull with one beautiful, long, curling horn. We found the other horn below in the grass and I screwed it back onto its bone base.

"Shenzi," M'Cola said and imitated a man pulling a bow. The skull was quite clean but the hollow horns had some damp residue in them, smelled unbearably foul and, giving no sign of having noticed the stench, I handed them to Garrick who promptly, without sign, gave them to Abdullah. Abdullah wrinkled the edge of his flat nose and shook his head. They really smelled abominably. M'Cola and I grinned and Garrick looked virtuous.

I decided a good idea might be to drive along the road in the car, watching for kudu, and hunt any likely-looking clearings. We went back to the car and did this, working several clearings with no luck. By then the sun was up and the road was becoming populous with travellers, both white-clothed and naked, and we decided to head for camp. On our way in, we stopped and stalked the other salt lick. There was an impalla on it looking very red where the sun struck his hide in the patches between the gray trees and there were many kudu tracks. We smoothed them over and drove on in to camp to find a sky full of locusts passing over, going to the westward, making the sky, as you looked up, seem a pink dither of flickering passage, flickering like an old cinema film, but pink instead of gray. P. O. M. and Pop came out and were very disappointed. No rain had fallen in camp and they had been sure we would have something when we came in.

"Did my literary pal get off?"

"Yes," Pop said. "He's gone into Handeni."

"He told me all about American women," P. O. M. said. "Poor old Poppa, I was sure you'd get one. Damn the rain."

"How are American women?"

"He thinks they're terrible."

"Very sound fellow," said Pop. "Tell me just what happened today."

We sat in the shade of the dining tent and I told them.

"A Wanderobo," Pop said. "They're frightful shots. Bad luck."

"I thought it might be one of those travelling sportsmen you see with their bows slung going along the road.

He saw the lick by the road and trailed up to the other one."

"Not very likely. They carry those bows and arrows as protection. They're not hunters."

"Well, whoever it was put it on us."

"Bad luck. That, and the rain. I've had scouts out here on both the hills but they've seen nothing."

"Well, we're not bitched until tomorrow night. When do we have to leave?"

"After tomorrow."

"That bloody savage."

"I suppose Karl is blasting up the sable down there."

"We won't be able to get into camp for the horns. Have you heard anything?"

"No."

"I'm going to give up smoking for six months for you to get one," P. O. M. said. "I've started already."

We had lunch and afterwards I went into the tent and lay down and read. I knew we still had a chance on the lick in the morning and I was not going to worry about it. But I *was* worried and I did not want to go to sleep and wake up feeling dopey so I came out and sat in one of the canvas chairs under the open dining tent and read somebody's life of Charles the Second and looked up every once in a while to watch the locusts. The locusts were exciting to see and it was difficult for me to take them as a matter of course.

Finally I went to sleep in the chair with my feet on a

chop-box and when I woke there was Garrick, the bastard, wearing a large, very floppy, black and white ostrich-plume head-dress.

"Go away," I said in English.

He stood smirking proudly, then turned so I could see the head-dress from the side.

I saw Pop coming out of his tent with a pipe in his mouth. "Look what we have," I called to him.

He looked, said, "Christ," and went back into the tent.

"Come on," I said. "We'll just ignore it."

Pop came out, finally, with a book and we took no notice of Garrick's head-dress at all, sitting and talking, while he posed with it.

"Bastard's been drinking, too," I said.

"Probably."

"I can smell it."

Pop, without looking at him, spoke a few words to Garrick in a very soft voice.

"What did you tell him?"

"To go and get dressed properly and be ready to start."

Garrick walked off, his plumes waving.

"Not the moment for his bloody ostrich plumes," Pop said.

"Some people probably like them."

"That's it. Start photographing them."

"Awful," I said.

"Frightful," Pop agreed.

"On the last day if we don't get anything, I'm going to

shoot Garrick in the ass. What would that cost me?"

"Might make lots of trouble. If you shoot one, you have to shoot the other, too."

"Only Garrick."

"Better not shoot then. Remember it's me you get into trouble."

"Joking, Pop."

Garrick, un-head-dressed and with Abdullah, appeared and Pop spoke with them.

"They want to hunt around the hill a new way."

"Splendid. When?"

"Any time now. It looks like rain. You might get going."

I sent Molo for my boots and a raincoat, M'Cola came out with the Springfield; and we walked down to the car. It had been heavily cloudy all day although the sun had come through the clouds in the forenoon for a time and again at noon. The rains were moving up on us. Now it was starting to rain and the locusts were no longer flying.

"I'm dopey with sleep," I told Pop, "I'm going to have a drink."

We were standing under the big tree by the cooking fire with the light rain pattering in the leaves. M'Cola brought the whiskey flask and handed it to me very solemnly.

"Have one?"

"I don't see what harm it can do."

We both drank and Pop said, "The hell with them."

"The hell with them."

"You may find some bloody tracks."

"We'll run them out of the country."

In the car we turned to the right on the road, drove on up past the mud village and turned off the road to the left onto a red, hard, clay track that circled the edge of the hills and was close bordered on either side with trees. It was raining fairly hard now and we drove slowly. There seemed to be enough sand in the clay to keep the car from slipping. Suddenly, from the back seat, Abdullah, very excited, told Kamau to stop. We stopped with a skid, all got out, and walked back. There was a freshly cut kudu track in the wet clay. It could not have been made more than five minutes before as it was sharp-edged and the dirt, that had been picked up by the inside of the hoof, was not yet softened by the rain.

"Doumi," Garrick said and threw back his head and spread his arms wide to show horns that hung back over his withers. "Kubwa Sana!" Abdullah agreed it was a bull; a huge bull.

"Come on," I said.

It was easy tracking and we knew we were close. In rain or snow it is much easier to come up close to animals and I was sure we were going to get a shot. We followed the tracks through thick brush and then out into an open patch. I stopped to wipe the rain off my glasses and blew through the aperture in the rear sight of the Springfield. It was raining hard now, and I pulled my hat low down over my eyes to keep my glasses dry. We skirted the edge of the open patch and then, ahead, there was a crash and I saw a gray, white-striped animal making off through the brush. I threw the gun up and M'Cola grabbed my arm, "Manamouki!" he whispered. It was a cow kudu. But when we came up to where it had jumped there were no other tracks. The same tracks we had followed led, logically and with no possibility of doubt, from the road to that cow.

"Doumi Kubwa Sana!" I said, full of sarcasm and disgust to Garrick and made a gesture of giant horns flowing back from behind his ears.

"Manamouki Kubwa Sana," he said very sorrowfully and patiently. "What an enormous cow."

"You lousy ostrich-plumed punk," I told him in English. "Manamouki! Manamouki! Manamouki!"

"Manamouki," said M'Cola and nodded his head.

I got out the dictionary, couldn't find the words, and made it clear to M'Cola with signs that we would circle back in a long swing to the road and see if we could find another track. We circled back in the rain getting thoroughly soaked, saw nothing, found the car, and as the rain lessened and the road still seemed firm decided to go on until it was dark. Puffs of cloud hung on the hillside after the rain and the trees dripped but we saw nothing. Not in the open glades, not in the fields where the bush thinned, not on the green hillsides. Finally it was dark and we went back to camp. The Springfield was very wet when we got out of the car and I told M'Cola to clean it carefully and oil it well. He said he would and I went on and into the tent where a lantern was burning, took off my clothes, had a bath in the canvas tub and came out to the fire comfortable and relaxed in pyjamas, dressing gown and mosquito boots.

P. O. M. and Pop were sitting in their chairs by the fire and P. O. M. got up to make me a whiskey and soda.

"M'Cola told me," Pop said from his chair by the fire.

"A damned big cow," I told him. "I nearly busted her. What do you think about the morning?"

"The lick I suppose. We've scouts out to watch both of these hills. You remember that old man from the village? He's on a wild-goose chase after them in some country over beyond the hills. He and the Wanderobo. They've been gone three days."

"There's no reason why we shouldn't get one on the lick where Karl shot his. One day is as good as another."

"Quite."

"It's the last damned day though and the lick may be rained out. As soon as it's wet there's no salt. Just mud."

"That's it."

"I'd like to see one."

"When you do, take your time and make sure of him. Take your time and kill him."

"I don't worry about that."

"Let's talk about something else," P. O. M. said. "This makes me too nervous."

"I wish we had old Leather Pants," Pop said. "God, he was a talker. He made the old man here talk too. Give us that spiel on modern writers again."

"Go to hell."

"Why don't we have some intellectual life?" P. O. M. asked. "Why don't you men ever discuss world topics? Why am I kept in ignorance of everything that goes on?"

"World's in a hell of a shape," Pop stated.

"Awful."

"What's going on in America?"

"Damned if I know! Some sort of Y. M. C. A. show. Starry eyed bastards spending money that somebody will have to pay. Everybody in our town quit work to go on relief. Fishermen all turned carpenters. Reverse of the Bible."

"How are things in Turkey?"

"Frightful. Took the fezzes away. Hanged any amount of old pals. Ismet's still around though."

"Been in France lately?"

"Didn't like it. Gloomy as hell. Been a bad show there just now."

"By God," said Pop, "It must have been if you can believe the papers."

"When they riot they really riot. Hell, they've got a tradition."

"Were you in Spain for the revolution?"

"I got there late. Then we waited for two that didn't come. Then we missed another."

"Did you see the one in Cuba?"

"From the start."

"How was it?"

"Beautiful. Then lousy. You couldn't believe how lousy."

"Stop it," P. O. M. said. "I know about those things. I was crouched down behind a marble-topped table while they were shooting in Havana. They came by in cars shooting at everybody they saw. I took my drink with me and I was very proud not to have spilled it or forgotten it. The children said, 'Mother, can we go out in the afternoon to see the shooting?' They got so worked up about revolution we had to stop mentioning it. Bumby got so bloodthirsty about Mr. M. he had terrible dreams."

"Extraordinary," Pop said.

"Don't make fun of me. I don't want to just hear about revolutions. All we see or hear is revolutions. I'm sick of them."

"The old man must like them."

"I'm sick of them."

"You know, I've never seen one," Pop said.

"They're beautiful. Really. For quite a while. Then they go bad."

"They're very exciting," P. O. M. said. "I'll admit that. But I'm sick of them. Really, I don't care anything about them."

"I've been studying them a little."

"What did you find out?" Pop asked.

"They were all very different but there were some things you could co-ordinate. I'm going to try to write a study of them."

"It could be damned interesting."

"If you have enough material. You need an awful lot of past performances. It's very hard to get anything true on anything you haven't seen yourself because the ones that fail have such a bad press and the winners always lie so. Then you can only really follow anything in places where you speak the language. That limits you of course. That's why I would never go to Russia. When you can't overhear it's no good. All you get are handouts and sight-seeing. Any one who knows a foreign language in any country is damned liable to lie to you. You get your good dope always from the people and when you can't talk with people and can't overhear you don't get anything that's of anything but journalistic value."

"You want to knuckle down on your Swahili then."

"I'm trying to."

"Even then you can't overhear because they're always talking their own language."

"But if I ever write anything about this it will just be landscape painting until I know something about it. Your first seeing of a country is a very valuable one. Probably more valuable to yourself than to any one else, is the hell of it. But you ought to always write it to try to get it stated. No matter what you do with it."

"Most of the damned Safari books are most awful bloody bores."

"They're terrible."

"The only one I ever liked was Streeter's. What did he call it? Denatured Africa. He made you feel what it was like. That's the best."

"I liked Charlie Curtis's. It was very honest and it made a fine picture."

"That man Streeter was damned funny though. Do you remember when he shot the kongoni?"

"It was very funny."

"I've never read anything, though, that could make you feel about the country the way we feel about it. They all have this damned Nairobi fast life or else bloody rot about shooting beasts with horns half an inch longer than some one else shot. Or muck about danger."

"I'd like to try to write something about the country and the animals and what it's like to some one who knows nothing about it."

"Have a try at it. Can't do any harm. You know I wrote a diary of that Alaskan trip."

"I'd love to read it," P. O. M. said. "I didn't know you were a writer, Mr. J. P."

"No bloody fear," said Pop. "If you'd read it, though, I'll send for it. You know it's just what we did each day and how Alaska looked to an Englishman from Africa. It'd bore you."

"Not if you wrote it," P. O. M. said.

"Little woman's giving us compliments," Pop said.

"Not me. You."

"I've read things by him," she said. "I want to read what Mr. J. P. writes."

"Is the old man really a writer?" Pop asked her. "I haven't seen anything to prove it. You're sure he doesn't support you by tracking and wing shooting?"

"Oh, yes. He writes. When he's going well he's awfully easy to get along with. But just before he gets going he's frightful. His temper has to go bad before he can write. When he talks about never writing again I know he's about to get started."

"We ought to get more literary conversation from him," Pop said. "Leather Breeches was the lad. Give us some literary anecdotes."

"Well, the last night we were in Paris I'd been out shooting at Ben Gallagher's in the Sologne the day before and he had a *fermée,* you know, they put up a low fence while they're out feeding, and shot rabbits in the morning and in the afternoon we had several drives and shot pheasants and I shot a chevreuil."

"That isn't literary."

"Wait. The last night Joyce and his wife came to dinner and we had a pheasant and a quarter of the chevreuil with the saddle and Joyce and I got drunk because we were off for Africa the next day. God, we had a night."

"That's a hell of a literary anecdote," Pop said. "Who's Joyce?"

"Wonderful guy," I said. "Wrote *Ulysses.*"

"Homer wrote Ulysses," Pop said.

"Who wrote *Æschylus?*"

"Homer," said Pop. "Don't try to trap me. D'you know many more literary anecdotes?"

"Ever heard of Pound?"

"No," said Pop. "Absolutely no."

"I know some good ones about Pound."

"Suppose you and he ate some funny-sounding beast and then got drunk."

"Several times," I said.

"Literary life must be awfully jolly. Think I'd make a writer?"

"Rather."

"We're going to chuck all this," Pop told P. O. M., "and both be writers. Give us another anecdote."

"Ever heard of George Moore?"

"Chap that wrote 'But before I go, George Moore, here's a last long health to you?' "

"That's him."

"What about him."

"He's dead."

"That's a damned dismal anecdote. You can do better than that."

"I saw him in a book-shop once."

"That's better. See how lively he can make them?"

"I went to call on him once in Dublin," P. O. M. said, "With Clara Dunn."

"What happened?"

"He wasn't in."

"By God. I tell you the literary life's the thing," Pop said. "You can't beat it."

"I hate Clara Dunn," I said.

"So do I," said Pop. "What did she write?"

"Letters," I said. "You know Dos Passos?"

"Never heard of him."

"He and I used to drink hot kirsch in the winter time."

"What happened then?"

"People objected, finally."

"Only writer I ever met was Stewart Edward White," Pop said. "Used to admire his writing no end. Damned good, you know. Then I met him. Didn't like him."

"You're coming on," I said. "See. There's no trick to a literary anecdote."

"Why didn't you like him?" P. O. M. asked.

"Do I have to tell? Isn't the anecdote complete? It's just like the old man tells them."

"Go ahead and tell."

"Too much the old timer about him. Eyes used to vast distances and that sort of thing. Killed too many bloody lions. No credit kill so many lions. Gallop 'em, yes. Couldn't kill that many. Bloody lion kill you instead. Writes damned fine things in *The Saturday Evening Post* about what's the bloke's name, Andy Burnett. Oh, damned fine. Took an awful dislike to him, though. See him in Nairobi with his eyes used to vast distances. Wore his oldest clothes in town. Hell of a fine shot, everybody says."

"Why you're a literary bastard," I said. "Look at that for an anecdote."

"He's marvellous," P. O. M. said. "Aren't we ever going to eat?"

"Thought by God we'd eaten," Pop said. "Start these anecdotes. No end to 'em."

After dinner we sat by the fire a little while and then went to bed. One thing seemed to be on Pop's mind and before I went in the tent he said, "After you've waited so long, when you get a shot take it easy. You're fast enough so you can take your time, remember. Take it easy."

"All right."

"I'll have them get you up early."

"All right. I'm plenty sleepy."

"Good night, Mr. J. P.," P. O. M. called from the tent.

"Good night," Pop said. He moved toward his tent carrying himself with comic stiffness, walking in the dark as carefully as though he were an opened bottle.

CHAPTER

MOLO waked me by pulling on the blanket in the morning and I was dressing, dressed, and out washing the sleep out of my eyes before I was really awake. It was still very dark and I could see Pop's back shadowed against the fire. I walked over holding the early morning cup of hot tea and milk in my hand waiting for it to be cool enough to drink.

"Morning," I said.

"Morning," he answered in that husky whisper.

"Sleep?"

"Very well. Feeling fit?"

"Sleepy is all."

I drank the tea and spat the leaves into the fire.

ELEVEN

"Tell your bloody fortune with those," Pop said.

"No fear."

Breakfast in the dark with a lantern, cool juice-slippery apricots, hash, hot-centered, brown, and catsup spread, two fried eggs and the warm promise-keeping coffee. On the third cup Pop, watching, smoking his pipe, said, "Too early for me to face it yet."

"Get you?"

"A little."

"I'm getting exercise," I said. "It doesn't bother me."

"Bloody anecdotes," Pop said. "Memsahib must think we're silly buggars."

"I'll think up some more."

"Nothing better than drinking. Don't know why it should make you feel bad."

"Are you bad?"

"Not too."

"Take a spot of Enos?"

"It's this damned riding in cars."

"Well, today's the day."

"Remember to take it very easy."

"You're not worried about that, are you?"

"Just a touch."

"Don't. It never worries me a minute. Truly."

"Good. Better get going."

"Have to make a trip first."

Standing in front of the canvas circle of the latrine I looked, as each morning, at that fuzzy blur of stars that the romanticists of astronomers called the Southern Cross. Each morning at this moment I observed the Southern Cross in solemn ceremony.

Pop was at the car. M'Cola handed me the Springfield and I got in the front. The tragedian and his tracker were in the back. M'Cola climbed in with them.

"Good luck," Pop said. Some one was coming from toward the tents. It was P. O. M. in her blue robe and mosquito boots. *"Oh,* good luck," she said. *"Please,* good luck."

I waved and we started, the headlights showing the way to the road.

There was nothing on the salt when we came up to it

after leaving the car about three miles away and making a very careful stalk. Nothing came all morning. We sat with our heads down in the blind, each covering a different direction through openings in the thatched withes, and always I expected the miracle of a bull kudu coming majestic and beautiful through the open scrub to the gray, dusty opening in the trees where the salt lick was worn, grooved, and trampled. There were many trails to it through the trees and on any one a bull might come silently. But nothing came. When the sun was up and we were warmed after the misty cold of the morning I settled my rump deeper in the dust and lay back against the wall of the hole, resting against the small of my back and my shoulders and still able to see out through the slit in the blind. Putting the Springfield across my knees I noticed that there was rust on the barrel. Slowly I pulled it along and looked at the muzzle. It was freshly brown with rust.

"The bastard never cleaned it last night after that rain," I thought and, very angry, I lifted the lug and slipped the bolt out. M'Cola was watching me with his head down. The other two were looking out through the blind. I held the rifle in one hand for him to look through the breech and then put the bolt back in and shoved it forward softly, lowering it with my finger on the trigger so that it was ready to cock rather than keeping it on the safety.

M'Cola had seen the rusty bore. His face had not

changed and I had said nothing but I was full of contempt and there had been indictment, evidence, and condemnation without a word being spoken. So we sat there, he with his head bent so only the bald top showed, me leaning back and looking out through the slit, and we were no longer partners, no longer good friends; and nothing came to the salt.

At ten o'clock the breeze, which had come up in the east, began to shift around and we knew it was no use. Our scent was being scattered in all directions around the blind as sure to frighten any animals as though we were revolving a searchlight in the dark. We got up out of the blind and went over to look in the dust of the lick for tracks. The rain had moistened it but it was not soaked and we saw several kudu tracks, probably made early in the night and one big bull track, long, narrow, heart-shaped; clearly, deeply cut.

We took the track and followed it on the damp reddish earth for two hours in thick bush that was like second-growth timber at home. Finally we had to leave it in stuff we could not move through. All this time I was angry about the uncleaned rifle and yet happy and eager with anticipation that we might jump the bull and get a snap at him in the brush. But we did not see him and now, in the big heat of noon, we made three long circles around some hills and finally came out into a meadow full of little, humpy Masai cattle and, leaving all shade behind, trailed back across the open country under the noon sun to the car.

Kamau, sitting in the car, had seen a kudu bull pass a hundred yards away. He was headed toward the salt lick at about nine o'clock when the wind began to be tricky, had evidently caught our scent and gone back into the hills. Tired, sweating, and feeling more sunk than angry now, I got in beside Kamau and we headed the car toward camp. There was only one evening left now, and no reason to expect we would have any better luck than we were having. As we came to camp, and the shade of the heavy trees cool as a pool, I took the bolt out of the Springfield and handed the rifle, boltless, to M'Cola without speaking or looking at him. The bolt I tossed inside the opening of our tent onto my cot.

Pop and P. O. M. were sitting under the dining tent.

"No luck?" Pop asked gently.

"Not a damn bit. Bull went by the car headed toward the salt. Must have spooked off. We hunted all over hell."

"Didn't you see anything?" P. O. M. asked. "Once we thought we heard you shoot."

"That was Garrick shooting his mouth off. Did the scouts get anything?"

"Not a thing. We've been watching both hills."

"Hear from Karl?"

"Not a word."

"I'd like to have seen one," I said. I was tired out and slipping into bitterness fast. "God damn them. What the hell did he have to blow that lick to hell for the first morning and gut-shoot a lousy bull and chase him all over the son-of-a-bitching country spooking it to holy bloody hell?"

"Bastards," said P. O. M., staying with me in my unreasonableness. "Sonsabitches."

"You're a good girl," I said. "I'm all right. Or I will be."

"It's been awful," she said. "Poor old Poppa."

"You have a drink," Pop said. "That's what you need."

"I've hunted them hard, Pop. I swear to God I have. I've enjoyed it and I haven't worried up until today. I was so damned sure. Those damned tracks all the time —what if I never see one? How the hell do I know we can ever get back here again?"

"You'll be back," Pop said. "You don't have to worry about that. Go ahead. Drink it."

"I'm just a lousy belly-aching bastard but I swear they haven't gotten on my nerves until today."

"Belly-ache," said Pop. "Better to get it out."

"What about lunch?" asked P. O. M. "Aren't you frightfully hungry?"

"The hell with lunch. The thing is, Pop, we've never seen them on the salt in the evening and we've never seen a bull in the hills. I've only got tonight. It looks washed up. Three times I've had them cold and Karl and the Austrian and the Wanderobo beat us."

"We're not beaten," said Pop. "Drink another one of those."

We had lunch, a very good lunch, and it was just over when Kati came and said there was some one to see Pop. We could see their shadows on the tent fly, then they came around to the front of the tent. It was the old man of the first day, the old farmer, but now he was gotten up as a hunter and carried a long bow and a sealed quiver of arrows.

He looked older, more disreputable and tired-er than ever and his get-up was obviously a disguise. With him was the skinny, dirty, Wanderobo with the slit and curled-up ears who stood on one leg and scratched the back of his knee with his toes. His head was on one side and he had a narrow, foolish, and depraved-looking face.

The old man was talking earnestly to Pop, looking him in the eye and speaking slowly, without gestures.

"What's he done? Gotten himself up like that to get some of the scout money?" I asked.

"Wait," Pop said.

"Look at the pair of them," I said. "That goofy Wanderobo and that lousy old fake. What's he say, Pop?"

"He hasn't finished," Pop said.

Finally the old man was finished and he stood there leaning on his property bow. They both looked very tired but I remember thinking they looked a couple of disgusting fakes.

"He says," Pop began, "They have found a country

where there are kudu and sable. He has been there three days. They know where there is a big kudu bull and he has a man watching him now."

"Do you believe it?" I could feel the liquor and the fatigue drain out of me and the excitement come in.

"God knows," said Pop.

"How far away is the country?"

"One day's march. I suppose that's three or four hours in the car if the car can go."

"Does he think the car can get in?"

"None ever has been in but he thinks you can make it."

"When did they leave the man watching the kudu?"

"This morning."

"Where are the sable?"

"There in the hills."

"How do we get in?"

"I can't make out except that you cross the plain, go around that mountain and then south. He says no one has ever hunted there. He hunted there when he was young."

"Do you believe it?"

"Of course natives lie like hell, but he tells it very straight."

"Let's go."

"You'd better start right away. Go as far as you can in the car and then use it for a base and hunt on from there. The Memsahib and I will break camp in the morning, move the outfit and go on to where Dan and Mr. T.

are. Once the outfit is over that black cotton stretch we're all right if the rain catches us. You come on and join us. If you're caught we can always send the car back by Kandoa, if worst comes, and the trucks down to Tanga and around."

"Don't you want to come?"

"No. You're better off alone on a show like this. The more people the less game you'll see. You should hunt kudu alone. I'll move the outfit and look after the little Memsahib."

"All right," I said. "And I don't have to take Garrick or Abdullah?"

"Hell, no. Take M'Cola, Kamau and these two. I'll tell Molo to pack your things. Go light as hell."

"God damn it, Pop. Do you think it could be true?"

"Maybe," said Pop. "We have to play it."

"How do you say sable?"

"Tarahalla."

"Valhalla, I can remember. Do the females have horns?"

"Sure, but you can't make a mistake. The bull is black and they're brown. You can't go wrong."

"Has M'Cola ever seen one?"

"I don't think so. You've got four on your license. Any time you can better one, go ahead."

"Are they hard to kill?"

"They're tough. They're not like a kudu. If you've got one down be careful how you walk up to him."

"What about time?"

"We've got to get out. Make it back tomorrow night if you can. Use your own judgment. I think this is the turning point. You'll get a kudu."

"Do you know what it's like?" I said. "It's just like when we were kids and we heard about a river no one had ever fished out on the huckleberry plains beyond the Sturgeon and the Pigeon."

"How did the river turn out?"

"Listen. We had a hell of a time to get in and the night we got there, just before dark, and saw it, there was a deep pool and a long straight stretch and the water so cold you couldn't keep your hand in it and I threw a cigarette butt in and a big trout hit it and they kept snapping it up and spitting it out as it floated until it went to pieces."

"Big trout?"

"The biggest kind."

"God save us," said Pop. "What did you do then?"

"Rigged up my rod and made a cast and it was dark and there was a nighthawk swooping around and it was cold as a bastard and then I was fast to three fish the second the flies hit the water."

"Did you land them?"

"The three of them."

"You damned liar."

"I swear to God."

"I believe you. Tell me the rest when you come back. Were they big trout?"

"The biggest bloody kind."

"God save us," said Pop. "You're going to get a kudu. Get started."

In the tent I found P. O. M. and told her.

"Not really?"

"Yes."

"Hurry up," she said. "Don't talk. Get started."

I found raincoat, extra boots, socks, bathrobe, bottle of quinine tablets, citronella, notebook, a pencil, my solids, the cameras, the emergency kit, knife, matches, extra shirt and undershirt, a book, two candles, money, the flask——

"What else?"

"Have you got soap? Take a comb and a towel. Got handkerchiefs?"

"All right."

Molo had everything packed in a ruck-sack and I found my field glasses, M'Cola taking Pop's big field glasses, a canteen with water and Kati sending a chop-box with food. "Take plenty of beer," Pop said. "You can leave it in the car. We're short on whiskey but there's a bottle."

"How will that leave you?"

"All right. There's more at the other camp. We sent two bottles on with Mr. K."

"I'll only need the flask," I said. "We'll split the bottle."

"Take plenty of beer then. There's any amount of it."

"What's the bastard doing?" I said, pointing at Garrick who was getting into the car.

"He says you and M'Cola won't be able to talk with the natives there. You'll have to have some one to interpret."

"He's poison."

"You *will* need some one to interpret whatever they speak into Swahili."

"All right. But tell him he's not running the show and to keep his bloody mouth shut."

"We'll go to the top of the hill with you," Pop said and we started off, the Wanderobo hanging to the side of the car. "Going to pick the old man up in the village."

Every one in camp was out to watch us go.

"Have we got plenty of salt?"

"Yes."

Now we were standing by the car on the road in the village waiting for the old man and Garrick to come back from their huts. It was early afternoon and the sky was clouding over and I was looking at P. O. M., very desirable, cool, and neat-looking in her khaki and her boots, her Stetson on one side of her head, and at Pop, big, thick, in the faded corduroy sleeveless jacket that was almost white now from washing and the sun.

"You be a good girl."

"Don't ever worry. I wish I could go."

"It's a one-man show," Pop said. "You want to get in

fast and do the dirty and get out fast. You've a big load as it is."

The old man appeared and got into the back of the car with M'Cola who was wearing my old khaki sleeveless, quail-shooting coat.

"M'Cola's got the old man's coat," Pop said.

"He likes to carry things in the game pockets," I said.

M'Cola saw we were talking about him. I had forgotten about the uncleaned rifle. Now I remembered it and said to Pop, "Ask him where he got the new coat."

M'Cola grinned and said something.

"He says it is his property."

I grinned at him and he shook his old bald head and it was understood that I had said nothing about the rifle.

"Where's that bastard Garrick?" I asked.

Finally he came with his blanket and got in with M'Cola and the old man behind. The Wanderobo sat with me in front beside Kamau.

"That's a lovely-looking friend you have," P. O. M. said. "You be good too."

I kissed her good-bye and we whispered something.

"Billing and cooing," Pop said. "Disgusting."

"Good-bye, you old bastard."

"Good-bye, you damned bullfighter."

"Good-bye, sweet."

"Good-bye and good luck."

"You've plenty of petrol and we'll leave some here," Pop called.

I waved and we were starting down hill through the village on a narrow track that led down and onto the scrubby dry plain that spread out below the two great blue hills.

I looked back as we went down the hill and saw the two figures, the tall thick one and the small neat one, each wearing big Stetson hats, silhouetted on the road as they walked back toward camp, then I looked ahead at the dried-up, scrubby plain.

GREEN HILLS OF AFRICA

PART IV

Pursuit as Happiness

CHAPTER

THE road was only a track and the plain was very discouraging to see. As we went on we saw a few thin Grant's gazelles showing white against the burnt yellow of the grass and the gray trees. My exhilaration died with the stretching out of this plain, the typical poor game country, and it all began to seem very impossible and romantic and quite untrue. The Wanderobo had a very strong odor and I looked at the way the lobes of his ears were stretched and then neatly wrapped on themselves and at his strange un-negroid, thin-lipped face. When he saw me studying his face he smiled pleasantly and scratched his chest. I looked around at the back of

TWELVE

the car. M'Cola was asleep. Garrick was sitting straight up, dramatizing his awakeness, and the old man was trying to see the road.

By now there was no more road, only a cattle track, but we were coming to the edge of the plain. Then the plain was behind us and ahead there were big trees and we were entering a country the loveliest that I had seen in Africa. The grass was green and smooth, short as a meadow that has been mown and is newly grown, and the trees were big, high-trunked, and old with no undergrowth but only the smooth green of the turf like a deer park and we drove on through shade and patches of sunlight following a faint trail the Wanderobo pointed out. I could not believe we had suddenly come to any such wonderful country. It was a country to wake from, happy to have had the dream and, seeing if it would clown away, I reached up and touched the Wanderobo's ear. He jumped and Kamau snickered. M'Cola nudged me from the back seat and pointed and there, standing in an open space between the trees, his head up, staring at us, the bristles on his back erect, long, thick, white tusks up-curving, his eyes showing bright, was a very large wart-hog boar watching us from less than twenty yards. I motioned to Kamau to stop and we sat looking at him and he at us. I put the rifle up and sighted on his chest. He watched and did not move. Then I motioned to Kamau to throw in the clutch and we went on and made a curve to the right and left the wart-hog, who had never moved, nor showed any fright at seeing us.

I could see that Kamau was excited and, looking back, M'Cola nodded his head up and down in agreement. None of us had ever seen a wart-hog that would not bolt off, fast-trotting, tail in air. This was a virgin country, an un-hunted pocket in the million miles of bloody Africa. I was ready to stop and make camp anywhere.

This was the finest country I had seen but we went on, winding along through the big trees over the softly rolling grass. Then ahead and to the right we saw the high stockade of a Masai village. It was a very large village and out of it came running long-legged, brown, smooth-moving men who all seemed to be of the same age and who wore their hair in a heavy club-like queue that swung against their shoulders as they ran. They came up to the car and surrounded it, all laughing and smiling and talking. They all were tall, their teeth were white and good, and their hair was stained a red brown and arranged in a looped fringe on their foreheads. They carried spears and they were very handsome and extremely jolly, not sullen, nor contemptuous like the northern Masai, and they wanted to know what we were going to do. The Wanderobo evidently said we were hunting kudu and were in a hurry. They had the car surrounded so we could not move. One said something and three or four others joined in and Kamau explained to me that they had seen two kudu bulls go along the trail in the afternoon.

"It can't be true," I said to myself. "It can't be."

I told Kamau to start and slowly we pushed through them, they all laughing and trying to stop the car, making it all but run over them. They were the tallest, best-built, handsomest people I had ever seen and the first truly light-hearted happy people I had seen in Africa. Finally, when we were moving, they started to run beside the car smiling and laughing and showing how easily they could run and then, as the going was better, up the smooth valley of a stream, it became a contest and one after another dropped out of the running, waving and smiling as they left until there were only two still running with us, the finest runners of the lot, who kept pace easily with the car as they moved long-legged, smoothly, loosely, and with pride. They were running too, at the pace of a fast miler, and carrying their spears as well. Then we had to turn to the right and climb out of the putting-green smoothness of the valley into a rolling meadow and, as we slowed, climbing in first gear, the whole pack came up again, laughing and trying not to seem winded. We went through a little knot of brush and a small rabbit started out, zig-zagging wildly and all the Masai behind now in a mad sprint. They caught the rabbit and the tallest runner came up with him to the car and handed him to me. I held him and could feel the thumping of his heart through the soft, warm, furry body, and as I stroked him the Masai patted my arm. Holding him by the ears I handed him back. No, no, he was mine. He was a present. I handed him to M'Cola. 'Cola did not take him seriously and handed him to one of the Masai. We were moving and they were running again now. The Masai stooped and put the rabbit on the ground and as he ran free they all laughed. M'Cola shook his head. We were all very impressed by these Masai.

"Good Masai," M'Cola said, very moved. "Masai many cattle. Masai no kill to eat. Masai kill man."

The Wanderobo patted himself on the chest.

"Wanderobo—Masai," he said, very proudly, claiming kin. His ears were curled in the same way theirs were. Seeing them running and so damned handsome and so happy made us all happy. I had never seen such quick disinterested friendliness, nor such fine looking people.

"*Good* Masai," M'Cola repeated, nodding his head emphatically. "*Good, good* Masai." Only Garrick seemed impressed in a different way. For all his khaki clothes and his letter from B'wana Simba, I believe these Masai frightened him in a very old place. They were our friends, not his. They certainly were our friends though. They had that attitude that makes brothers, that unexpressed but instant and complete acceptance that you must be Masai wherever it is you come from. That attitude you only get from the best of the English, the best of the Hungarians and the very best Spaniards; the thing that used to be the most clear distinction of nobility when there was nobility. It is an ignorant attitude and the people who have it do not survive, but very few pleasanter things ever happen to you than the encountering of it.

So now there were only the two of them left again, running, and it was hard going and the machine was beating them. They were still running well and still loose and long but the machine was a cruel pacemaker. So I told Kamau to speed it up and get it over with because a sudden burst of speed was not the humiliation of a steady using. They sprinted, were beaten, laughed, and then we were leaning out, waving, and they stood leaning on their spears and waved. We were still great friends but now we were alone again and there was no track, only the general direction to follow around clumps of trees and along the run of this green valley.

After a little the trees grew closer and we left the idyllic country behind and now were picking our way along a faint trail through thick second-growth. Sometimes we came to a dead halt and had to get out and pull a log out of the way or cut a tree that blocked the body of the car. Sometimes we had to back out of bush and look for a way to circle around and come upon the trail again, chopping our way through with the long brush knives that are called pangas. The Wanderobo was a pitiful chopper and Garrick was little better. M'Cola did everything well in which a knife was used and he swung a panga with a fast yet heavy and vindictive stroke. I used it badly. There was too much wrist in it to learn it quickly; your wrist tired and the blade seemed to have a weight it did not have. I wished that I had a Michigan double-bitted ax, honed razor-sharp, to chop with instead of this sabering of trees.

Chopping through when we were stopped, avoiding all we could, Kamau driving with intelligence and a sound feeling for the country, we came through the difficult going and out into another open-meadow stretch and could see a range of hills off to our right. But here there had been a recent heavy rain and we had to be very careful about the low parts of the meadow where the tires cut in through the turf to mud and

spun in the slick greasiness. We cut brush and shov-
elled out twice and then, having learned not to trust any
low part, we skirted the high edge of the meadow and
then were in timber again. As we came out, after several
long circles in the woods to find places where we could
get the car through, we were on the bank of a stream,
where there was a sort of brushy bridging across the bed
built like a beaver dam and evidently designed to hold
back the water. On the other side was a thorn-brush-
fenced cornfield, a steep, stump-scattered bank with corn
planted all over it, and some abandoned looking corrals
or thorn-bush-fenced enclosures with mud and stick
buildings and to the right there were cone-shaped grass
huts projecting above a heavy thorn fence. We all got
out, for this stream was a problem and, on the other side,
the only place we could get up the bank led through the
stump-filled maize field.

The old man said the rain had come that day. There
had been no water going over the brushy dam when they
had passed that morning. I was feeling fairly depressed.
Here we had come through a beautiful country of virgin
timber where kudu had been seen walking along the trail
to end up stuck on the bank of a little creek in some one's
cornfield. I had not expected any cornfield and I resented
it. I thought we would have to get permission to drive
through the maize, provided we could make it across the
stream and up the bank and I took off my shoes and
waded across the stream to test it underfoot. The brush

and saplings on the bottom were packed hard and firm and I was sure we could cross if we took it fairly fast. M'Cola and Kamau agreed and we walked up the bank to see how it would be. The mud of the bank was soft but there was dry earth underneath and I figured we could shovel our way up if we could get through the stumps. But we would need to unload before we tried it.

Coming toward us, from the direction of the huts, were two men and a boy. I said "Jambo," as they came up. They answered, "Jambo," and then the old man and the Wanderobo talked with them. M'Cola shook his head at me. He did not understand a word. I thought we were asking permission to go through the corn. When the old man finished talking the two men came closer and we shook hands.

They looked like no negroes I had ever seen. Their faces were a gray brown, the oldest looked to be about fifty, had thin lips, an almost Grecian nose, rather high cheekbones, and large, intelligent eyes. He had great poise and dignity and seemed to be very intelligent. The younger man had the same cast of features and I took him for a younger brother. He looked about thirty-five. The boy was as pretty as a girl and looked rather shy and stupid. I had thought he was a girl from his face for an instant when he first came up, as they all wore a sort of Roman toga of unbleached muslin gathered at the shoulder that revealed no line of their bodies.

They were talking with the old man, who, now that

I looked at him standing with them, seemed to bear a sort of wrinkled and degenerate resemblance to the classic-featured owner of the shamba; just as the Wanderobo-Masai was a shrivelled caricature of the handsome Masai we had met in the forest.

Then we all went down to the stream and Kamau and I rigged ropes around the tires to act as chains while the Roman elder and the rest unloaded the car and carried the heaviest things up the steep bank. Then we crossed in a wild, water-throwing smash and, all pushing heavily, made it halfway up the bank before we stuck. We chopped and dug out and finally made it to the top of the bank but ahead was that maize field and I could not figure where we were to go from there.

"Where do we go?" I asked the Roman elder.

They did not understand Garrick's interpreting and the old man made the question clear.

The Roman pointed toward the heavy thorn-bush fence to the left at the edge of the woods.

"We can't get through there in the car."

"Campi," said M'Cola, meaning we were going to camp there.

"Hell of a place," I said.

"Campi," M'Cola said firmly and they all nodded.

"Campi! Campi!" said the old man.

"There we camp," Garrick announced pompously.

"You go to hell," I told him cheerfully.

I walked toward the camp site with the Roman who

was talking steadily in a language I could not understand a word of. M'Cola was with me and the others were loading and following with the car. I was remembering that I had read you must never camp in abandoned native quarters because of ticks and other hazards and I was preparing to hold out against this camp. We entered a break in the thorn-bush fence and inside was a building of logs and saplings stuck in the ground and crossed with branches. It looked like a big chicken coop. The Roman made us free of this and of the enclosure with a wave of his hand and kept on talking.

"Bugs," I said to M'Cola in Swahili, speaking with strong disapproval.

"No," he said, dismissing the idea. "No bugs."

"Bad bugs. Many bugs. Sickness."

"No bugs," he said firmly.

The no-bugs had it and with the Roman talking steadily, I hoped on some congenial topic, the car came up, stopped under a huge tree about fifty yards from the thorn-bush fence and they all commenced carrying the necessities in for the making of camp. My ground-sheet tent was slung between a tree and one side of the chicken coop and I sat down on a petrol case to discuss the shooting situation with the Roman, the old man, and Garrick while Kamau and M'Cola fixed up a camp and the Wanderobo-Masai stood on one leg and let his mouth hang open.

"Where were kudu?"

"Back there," waving his arm.

"Big ones?"

Arms spread to show hugeness of horns and a torrent from the Roman.

Me, dictionary-ing heavily, "Where was the one they were watching?"

No results on this but a long speech from the Roman which I took to mean they were watching them all.

It was late afternoon now and the sky was heavy with clouds. I was wet to the waist and my socks were mud soaked. Also I was sweating from pushing on the car and from chopping.

"When do we start?" I asked.

"Tomorrow," Garrick answered without bothering to question the Roman.

"No," I said. "Tonight."

"Tomorrow," Garrick said. "Late now. One hour light." He showed me one hour on my watch.

I dictionaried. "Hunt tonight. Last hour best hour."

Garrick implied that the kudu were too far away. That it was impossible to hunt and return, all this with gestures, "Hunt tomorrow."

"You bastard," I said in English. All this time the Roman and the old man had been standing saying nothing. I shivered. It was cold with the sun under the clouds in spite of the heaviness of the air after rain.

"Old man," I said.

"Yes, Master," said the old man. Dictionary-ing carefully, I said, "Hunt kudu tonight. Last hour best hour. Kudu close?"

"Maybe."

"Hunt now?"

They talked together.

"Hunt tomorrow," Garrick put in.

"Shut up, you actor," I said. "Old man. Little hunt now?"

"Yes," said old man and Roman nodded. "Little while."

"Good," I said and went to find a shirt and undershirt and a pair of socks.

"Hunt now," I told M'Cola.

"Good," he said. "M'uzuri."

With the clean feeling of dry shirt, fresh socks and a change of boots I sat on the petrol case and drank a whiskey and water while I waited for the Roman to come back. I felt certain I was going to have a shot at kudu and I wanted to take the edge off so I would not be nervous. Also I wanted not to catch a cold. Also I wanted the whiskey for itself, because I loved the taste of it and because, being as happy as I could be, it made me feel even better.

I saw the Roman coming and I pulled the zippers up on my boots, checked the cartridges in the magazine of the Springfield, took off the foresight protector and blew through the rear aperture. Then I drank what was left in the tin cup that was on the ground by the box and stood up, checking that I had a pair of handkerchiefs in my shirt pockets.

M'Cola came carrying his knife and Pop's big glasses. "You stay here," I said to Garrick. He did not mind. He thought we were silly to go out so late and he was glad to prove us wrong. The Wanderobo wanted to go.

"That's plenty," I said and waved the old man back and we started out of the corral with the Roman ahead, carrying a spear, then me, then M'Cola with glasses and the Mannlicher, full of solids, and last the Wanderobo-Masai with another spear.

It was after five when we struck off across the maize field and down to the stream, crossing where it narrowed in high grass a hundred yards above the dam and then, walking slowly and carefully, went up the grassy bank on the far side getting soaked to the waist as we stooped going through the wet grass and bracken. We had not been gone ten minutes and were moving carefully up the stream bank, when, without warning, the Roman grabbed my arm and pulled me bodily down to the ground as he crouched; me pulling back the bolt to cock the rifle as I dropped. Holding his breath he pointed and across the stream on the far bank at the edge of the trees was a large, gray animal, white stripes showing on his flanks and huge horns curling back from his head as he stood, broadside to us, head up, seeming to be listening. I raised the rifle but there was a bush in the way of the shot. I could not shoot over the bush without standing.

"Piga," whispered M'Cola. I shook my finger and commenced to crawl forward to be clear of the bush, sick afraid the bull would jump while I was trying to make the shot certain, but remembering Pop's "Take your time." When I saw I was clear I got on one knee, saw the bull through the aperture, marvelling at how big he looked and then, remembering not to have it matter, that it was the same as any other shot, I saw the bead centered exactly where it should be just below the top of the shoulder and squeezed off. At the roar he jumped and was going into the brush, but I knew I had hit him. I shot at a show of gray between the trees as he went in and M'Cola was shouting, "Piga! Piga!" meaning, "He's hit! He's hit!" and the Roman was slapping me on the shoulder, then he had his toga up around his neck and was running naked, and the four of us were running now, full speed, like hounds, splashing across the stream, tearing up the bank, the Roman ahead, crashing naked through the brush, then stooping and holding up a leaf with bright blood, slamming me on the back, M'Cola saying, "Damu! Damu!" blood, blood, then the deep cut tracks off to the right, me reloading, we all trailing in a dead run, it almost dark in the timber, the Roman, confused a moment by the trail, making a cast off to the right, then picking up blood once more, then pulling me down again with a jerk on my arm and none of us breathing as we saw him standing in a clearing a hundred yards

ahead, looking to me hard-hit and looking back, wide
ears spread, big, gray, white-striped, his horns a marvel,
as he looked straight toward us over his shoulder. I
thought I must make absolutely sure this time, now, with
the dark coming and I held my breath and shot him a
touch behind the fore-shoulder. We heard the bullet
smack and saw him buck heavily with the shot. M'Cola
shouted, "Piga! Piga! Piga!" as he went out of sight
and as we ran again, like hounds, we almost fell over
something. It was a huge, beautiful kudu bull, stone-
dead, on his side, his horns in great dark spirals, widespread and unbelievable as he lay dead five yards from
where we stood when I had just that instant shot. I
looked at him, big, long-legged, a smooth gray with the
white stripes and the great, curling, sweeping horns,
brown as walnut meats, and ivory pointed, at the big ears
and the great, lovely heavy-maned neck the white chevron
between his eyes and the white of his muzzle and I stooped
over and touched him to try to believe it. He was lying on
the side where the bullet had gone in and there was not a
mark on him and he smelled sweet and lovely like the
breath of cattle and the odor of thyme after rain.

Then the Roman had his arms around my neck and
M'Cola was shouting in a strange high sing-song voice
and Wanderobo-Masai kept slapping me on the shoulder
and jumping up and down and then one after the other
they all shook hands in a strange way that I had never
known in which they took your thumb in their fist and

held it and shook it and pulled it and held it again, while they looked you in the eyes, fiercely.

We all looked at him and M'Cola knelt and traced the curve of his horns with his finger and measured the spread with his arms and kept crooning, "Oo-oo-eee-eee," making small high noises of ecstasy and stroking the kudu's muzzle and his mane.

I slapped the Roman on the back and we went through the thumb pulling again; me pulling his thumb too. I embraced the Wanderobo-Masai and he, after a thumb-pulling of great intensity and feeling, slapped his chest and said very proudly, "Wanderobo-Masai wonderful guide."

"Wanderobo-Masai wonderful Masai," I said.

M'Cola kept shaking his head, looking at the kudu and making the strange small noises. Then he said, "Doumi, Doumi, Doumi! B'wana Kabor Kidogo, Kidogo." Meaning this was a bull of bulls. That Karl's had been a little one, a nothing.

We all knew we had killed the other kudu that I had mistaken for this one, while this first one was lying dead from the first shot, and it seemed of no importance beside the miracle of this kudu. But I wanted to see the other.

"Come on, kudu," I said.

"He's dead," said M'Cola, "Kufa!"

"Come on."

"This one best."

"Come on."

"Measure," M'Cola pleaded. I ran the steel tape around the curve of one horn, M'Cola holding it down. It was well over fifty inches. M'Cola looked at me anxiously.

"Big! Big!" I said. "Twice as big as B'wana Kabor."

"Eee-eee," he crooned.

"Come on," I said. The Roman was off already.

We cut for where we saw the bull when I shot and there were the tracks with blood breast high on the leaves in the brush from the start. In a hundred yards we came on him absolutely dead. He was not quite as big as the first bull. The horns were as long, but narrower, but he was as beautiful, and he lay on his side, bending down the brush where he fell.

We all shook hands again, using the thumb which evidently denoted extreme emotion.

"This askari," M'Cola explained. This bull was the policeman or bodyguard for the bigger one. He had evidently been in the timber when we had seen the first bull, had run with him, and had looked back to see why the big bull did not follow.

I wanted pictures and told M'Cola to go back to camp with the Roman and bring the two cameras, the Graflex and the cinema camera and my flashlight. I knew we were on the same side of the stream and above the camp and I hoped the Roman could make a short cut and get back before the sun set.

They went off and now, at the end of the day, the sun

came out brightly below the clouds and the Wanderobo-Masai and I looked at this kudu, measured his horns, smelled the fine smell of him, sweeter than an eland, even, stroked his nose, his neck, and his shoulder, marvelling at the great ears, and the smoothness and cleanness of his hide, looked at his hooves, that were built long, narrow, and springy so he seemed to walk on tip-toe, felt under his shoulder for the bullet-hole and then shook hands again while the Wanderobo-Masai told what a man he was and I told him he was my pal and gave him my best four-bladed pocket knife.

"Let's go look at the first one, Wanderobo-Masai," I said in English.

The Wanderobo-Masai nodded, understanding perfectly, and we trailed back to where the big one lay in the edge of the little clearing. We circled him, looking at him and then the Wanderobo-Masai, reaching underneath while I held the shoulder up, found the bullet hole and put his finger in. Then he touched his forehead with the bloody finger and made the speech about "Wanderobo-Masai wonderful guide!"

"Wanderobo-Masai king of guides," I said. "Wanderobo-Masai my pal."

I was wet through with sweat and I put on my raincoat that M'Cola had been carrying and left behind and turned the collar up around my neck. I was watching the sun now and worrying about it being gone before they got up with the cameras. In a little while we could hear them coming in the brush and I shouted to let them know where we were. M'Cola answered and we shouted back and forth and I could hear them talking and crashing in the brush while I would shout and watch the sun which was almost down. Finally I saw them and I shouted to M'Cola, "Run, run," and pointed to the sun, but there was no run left in them. They had made a fast trip uphill, through heavy brush, and when I got the camera, opened the lens wide and focused on the bull the sun was only lighting the tops of the trees. I took a half a dozen exposures and used the cinema while they all dragged the kudu to where there seemed to be a little more light, then the sun was down and, obligation to try to get a picture over, I put the camera into its case and settled, happily, with the darkness into the unresponsibility of victory; only emerging to direct M'Cola in where to cut to make a full enough cape when skinning out the head-skin. M'Cola used a knife beautifully and I liked to watch him skin-out, but tonight, after I had shown him where to make the first cut, well down on the legs, around the lower chest where it joined the belly and well back over the withers I did not watch him because I wanted to remember the bull as I had first seen him, so I went, in the dusk, to the second kudu and waited there until they came, with the flashlight and then, remembering that I had skinned-out or seen skinned-out every animal that I had ever shot, yet remembered every one exactly as he was at every moment, that one memory does not destroy another, and that the not-watching idea was only laziness and a form of putting the dishes in the sink until morning, I held the flashlight for M'Cola while he worked on the second bull and, although tired, enjoyed as always his fast, clean, delicate scalpeling with the knife, until, the cape all clear and spread back he nocked through the connection of the skull and the spine and then, twisting with the horns, swung the head loose and lifted it, cape and all, free from the neck, the cape hanging heavy and wet in the light of the electric torch that shone on his red hands and on the dirty khaki of his tunic. We left the Wanderobo-Masai, Garrick, the Roman, and his brother with a lantern to skin out and pack in the meat and M'Cola with a head, the old man with a head, and me with the flashlight and the two guns, we started in the dark back for camp.

In the dark the old man fell flat and M'Cola laughed; then the cape unrolled and came down over his face and he almost choked and we both laughed. The old man laughed too. Then M'Cola fell in the dark and the old man and I laughed. A little farther on I went through the covering on some sort of game pit and went flat on my face and got up to hear M'Cola chuckling and choking and the old man giggling.

"What the hell is this? A Chaplin comedy?" I asked them in English. They were both laughing under the heads. We got to the thorn-bush fence, finally, after a nightmare march through the brush and saw the fire at the camp and M'Cola seemed to be delighted when the old man fell going through the thorns and got up cursing and seeming barely able to lift the head as I shone the flash ahead of him to show him the opening.

We came up to the fire and I could see the old man's face bleeding as he put the head down against the stick and mud cabin. M'Cola put his head down, pointed at the old man's face and laughed and shook his head. I looked at the old man. He was completely done-in, his face was badly scratched, covered with mud and bleeding, and he was chuckling happily.

"B'wana fell down," M'Cola said and imitated me pitching forward. They both chuckled.

I made as though to take a swing at him and said, "Shenzi!"

He imitated me falling down again and then there was Kamau shaking hands very gently and respectfully and saying, "Good, B'wana! Very good, B'wana!" and then going over to the heads, his eyes shining and kneeling, stroking the horns and feeling the ears and crooning the same, sighing, "Ooo-ooo! Eee-eee!" noises M'Cola had made.

I went into the dark of the tent, we had left the lantern with the meat bringers, and washed, took off my wet clothes and feeling in the dark in my ruck-sack found a pair of pyjamas and a bath-robe. I came out to the fire wearing these and mosquito boots. I brought my wet things and my boots to the fire and Kamau spread them on sticks and put the boots, each one, leg-down, on a stick and back far enough from the blaze where the fire would not scorch them.

In the firelight I sat on a petrol box with my back against a tree and Kamau brought the whiskey flask and poured some in a cup and I added water from the canteen and sat drinking and looking in the fire, not thinking, in complete happiness, feeling the whiskey warm me and smooth me as you straighten the wrinkled sheet in a bed, while Kamau brought tins from the provisions to see what I would eat for supper. There were three tins of Christmas special mince meat, three tins of salmon, and three of mixed fruit, there were also a number of cakes of chocolate and a tin of Special Christmas Plum Pudding. I sent these back wondering what Kati had imagined the mince-meat to be. We had been looking for that plum pudding for two months.

"Meat?" I asked.

Kamau brought a thick, long chunk of roast Grant gazelle tenderloin from one of the Grant Pop had shot on the plain while we had been hunting the twenty-five-mile salt lick, and some bread.

"Beer?"

He brought one of the big German liter bottles and opened it.

It seemed too complicated sitting on the petrol case and I spread my raincoat on the ground in front of the fire where the ground had been dried by the heat and stretched my legs out, leaning my back against the wooden case. The old man was roasting meat on a stick. It was a choice piece he had brought with him wrapped in his toga. In a little while they all began to come in carrying meat and the hides and then I was stretched out drinking beer and watching the fire and all around they were talking and roasting meat on sticks. It was getting cold and the night was clear and there was the smell of the roasting meat, the smell of the smoke of the fire, the smell of my boots steaming, and, where he squatted close, the smell of the good old Wanderobo-Masai. But I could remember the odor of the kudu as he lay in the woods.

Each man had his own meat or collection of pieces of meat on sticks stuck around the fire, they turned them and tended them, and there was much talking. Two others that I had not seen had come over from the huts and the boy we had seen in the afternoon was with them. I was eating a piece of hot broiled liver I had lifted from one of the sticks of the Wanderobo-Masai and wondering where the kidneys were. The liver was delicious. I was wondering whether it was worth while getting up to get the dictionary to ask about the kidneys when M'Cola said, "Beer?"

"All right."

He brought the bottle, opened it, and I lifted it and drank half of it off to chase down that liver.

"It's a hell of a life," I told him in English.

He grinned and said, "More beer?" in Swahili.

My talking English to him was an acceptable joke.

"Watch," I said, and tipped the bottle up and let it all go down. It was an old trick we learned in Spain drinking out of wine skins without swallowing. This impressed the Roman greatly. He came over, squatted down by the raincoat and started to talk. He talked for a long time.

"Absolutely," I told him in English. "And furthermore he can take the sleigh."

"More beer?" M'Cola asked.

"You want to see the old man tight I suppose?"

"N'Dio," he said, "Yes," pretending to understand the English.

"Watch it, Roman," I started to let the beer go down, saw the Roman following the motion with his own throat, started to choke, barely recovered and lowered the bottle.

"That's all. Can't do it more than twice in an evening. Makes you liverish."

The Roman went on talking in his language. I heard him say Simba twice.

"Simba here?"

"No," he said. "Over there," waving at the dark, and I could not make out the story. But it sounded very good.

"Me plenty Simba," I said. "Hell of a man with Simba. Ask M'Cola." I could feel that I was getting the evening braggies but Pop and P. O. M. weren't here to listen. It was not nearly so satisfactory to brag when you could not be understood, still it was better than nothing. I definitely had the braggies, on beer, too.

"Amazing," I told the Roman. He went on with his own story. There was a little beer in the bottom of the bottle.

"Old Man," I said. "Mzee."

"Yes, B'wana," said the old man.

"Here's some beer for you. You're old enough so it can't hurt you."

I had seen the old man's eyes while he watched me drink and I knew he was another of the same. He took the bottle, drained it to the last bit of froth and crouched by his meat sticks holding the bottle lovingly.

"More beer?" asked M'Cola.

"Yes," I said. "And my cartridges."

The Roman had gone on steadily talking. He could tell a longer story even than Carlos in Cuba.

"That's mighty interesting," I told him. "You're a hell of a fellow, too. We're both good. Listen." M'Cola had brought the beer and my khaki coat with the cartridges in the pocket. I drank a little beer, noted the old man watching and spread out six cartridges. "I've got the braggies," I said. "You have to stand for this, look!" I touched each of the cartridges in turn, "Simba, Simba, Faro, Nyati, Tendalla, Tendalla. What do you think of that? You don't have to believe it. Look, M'Cola!" and I named the six cartridges again. "Lion, lion, rhino, buffalo, kudu, kudu."

"Ayee!" said the Roman excitedly.

"N'Dio," said M'Cola solemnly. "Yes, it is true."

"Ayee!" said the Roman and grabbed me by the thumb.

"God's truth," I said. "Highly improbable, isn't it?"

"N'Dio," said M'Cola, counting them over himself. "Simba, Simba, Faro, Nyati, Tendalla, Tendalla!"

"You can tell the others," I said in English. "That's a hell of a big piece of bragging. That'll hold me for to-night."

The Roman went on talking to me again and I listened carefully and ate another piece of the broiled liver. M'Cola was working on the heads now, skinning out one skull and showing Kamau how to skin out the easy part of the other. It was a big job to do for the two of them, working carefully around the eyes and the muzzle and the cartilage of the ears, and afterwards flesh all of the head skins so they would not spoil, and they were working at it very delicately and carefully in the firelight. I do not remember going to bed, nor if we went to bed.

I remember getting the dictionary and asking M'Cola to ask the boy if he had a sister and M'Cola saying, "No. No," to me very firmly and solemnly.

"Nothing tendacious, you understand. Curiosity."

M'Cola was firm. "No," he said and shook his head. "Hapana," in the same tone he used when we followed the lion into the sanseviera that time.

That disposed of the opportunities for social life and I looked up kidneys and the Roman's brother produced some from his lot and I put a piece between two pieces of liver on a stick and started it broiling.

"Make an admirable breakfast," I said out loud. "Much better than mince-meat."

Then we had a long talk about sable. The Roman did not call them Tarahalla and that name meant nothing to him. There was some confusion about buffalo because the Roman kept saying, "nyati," but he meant they were black like the buff. Then we drew pictures in the dust of ashes from the fire and what he meant were sable all right. The horns curved back like scimitars, way back over their withers.

"Bulls?" I said.

"Bulls and cows."

With the old man and Garrick interpreting, I believed I made out that there were two herds.

"Tomorrow."

"Yes," the Roman said. "Tomorrow."

" 'Cola," I said. "Today, kudu. Tomorrow, sable, buffalo, Simba."

"Hapana, buffalo!" he said and shook his head. "Hapana, Simba!"

"Me and the Wanderobo-Masai buffalo," I said.

"Yes," said the Wanderobo-Masai excitedly. "Yes."

"There are very big elephants near here," Garrick said.

"Tomorrow elephants," I said, teasing M'Cola.

"Hapana elephants!" he knew it was teasing but he did not even want to hear it said.

"Elephants," I said. "Buffalo, Simba, leopard."

The Wanderobo-Masai was nodding excitedly. "Rhino," he put in.

"Hapana!" M'Cola said shaking his head. He was beginning to suffer.

"In those hills many buffalo," the old man interpreted for the now very excited Roman who was standing and pointing beyond where the huts were.

"Hapana! Hapana! Hapana!" M'Cola said definitely and finally. "More beer?" putting down his knife.

"All right," I said. "I'm just kidding you."

M'Cola was crouched close talking, making an explanation. I heard Pop's title and I thought it was that Pop would not like it. That Pop would not want it.

"I was just kidding you," I said in English. Then in Swahili, "Tomorrow sable?"

"Yes," he said feelingly. "Yes."

After that the Roman and I had a long talk in which I spoke Spanish and he spoke whatever it was he spoke and I believe we planned the entire campaign for the next day.

CHAPTER

I DO not remember going to bed nor getting up, only being by the fire in the gray before daylight with a tin cup of hot tea in my hand and my breakfast, on the stick, not looking nearly so admirable and very overblown with ashes. The Roman was standing making an oration with gestures in the direction where the light was beginning to show and I remember wondering if the bastard had talked all night.

The head skins were all spread and neatly salted and the skulls with the horns were leaning against the log and stick house. M'Cola was folding the head skins. Kamau brought me the tins and I told him to open one

THIRTEEN

of fruit. It was cold from the night and the mixed fruit and the cold syrupy juice sucked down smoothly. I drank another cup of tea, went in the tent, dressed, put on my dry boots and we were ready to start. The Roman had said we would be back before lunch.

We had the Roman's brother as guide. The Roman was going, as near as I could make out, to spy on one of the herds of sable and we were going to locate the other. We started out with the brother ahead, wearing a toga and carrying a spear, then me with the Springfield slung and my small Zeiss glasses in my pocket, then M'Cola with Pop's glasses, slung on one side, water can-

247

teen on the other, skinning knife, whetstone, extra box of cartridges, and cakes of chocolates in his pockets, and the big gun over his shoulder, then the old man with the Graflex, Garrick with the movie camera, and the Wanderobo-Masai with a spear and bow and arrows.

We said good-bye to the Roman and started out of the thorn-bush fence just as the sun came through the gap in the hills and shone on the cornfield, the huts and the blue hills beyond. It promised to be a fine clear day.

The brother led the way through some heavy brush that soaked us all; then through the open forest, then steeply uphill until we were well up on the slope that rose behind the edge of the field where we were camped. Then we were on a good, smooth trail that graded back into these hills above which the sun had not yet risen. I was enjoying the early morning, still a little sleepy, going along a little mechanically and starting to think that we were a very big outfit to hunt quietly, although every one seemed to move quietly enough, when we saw two people coming toward us.

They were a tall, good-looking man with features like the Roman's, but slightly less noble, wearing a toga and carrying a bow and quiver of arrows, and behind him, his wife, very pretty, very modest, very wifely, wearing a garment of brown tanned skins and neck ornament of concentric copper wire circles and many wire circles on her arms and ankles. We halted, said "Jambo," and the brother talked to this seeming tribesman who had the air of a business man on the way downtown to his office and, as they spoke in rapid question and answer, I watched the most freshly brideful wife who stood a little in profile so that I saw her pretty pear-shaped breasts and the long, clean niggery legs and was studying her pleasant profile most profitably until her husband spoke to her suddenly and sharply, then in explanation and quiet command, and she moved around us, her eyes down, and went on along the trail that we had come, alone, we all watching her. The husband was going on with us, it seemed. He had seen the sable that morning and, slightly suspicious, obviously displeased at leaving that now out-of-sight wife of wives that we all had taken with our eyes, he led us off and to the right along another trail, well-worn and smooth, through woods that looked like fall at home and where you might expect to flush a grouse and have him whirr off to the other hill or pitch down in the valley.

So, sure enough we put up partridges and, watching them fly, I was thinking all the country in the world is the same country and all hunters are the same people. Then we saw a fresh kudu track beside the trail and then, as we moved through the early morning woods, no undergrowth now, the first sun coming through the tops of the trees, we came on the ever miracle of elephant tracks, each one as big around as the circle you make with your arms putting your hands together, and sunk a foot deep in the loam of the forest floor, where some bull had passed, travelling after rain. Looking at the way the tracks graded down through the pleasant forest I thought that we had the mammoths too, a long time ago, and when they travelled through the hills in southern Illinois they made these same tracks. It was just that we were an older country in America and the biggest game was gone.

We kept along the face of this hill on a pleasant sort of jutting plateau and then came out to the edge of the hill where there was a valley and a long open meadow with timber on the far side and a circle of hills at its upper end where another valley went off to the left. We stood in the edge of the timber on the face of this hill looking across the meadow valley which extended to the open out in a steep sort of grassy basin at the upper end where it was backed by the hills. To our left there were steep, rounded, wooded hills, with outcroppings of limestone rock that ran, from where we stood, up to the very head of the valley and there formed part of the other range of hills that headed it. Below us, to the right, the country was rough and broken in hills and stretches of meadow and then a steep fall of timber that ran to the blue hills we had seen to the westward beyond the huts where the Roman and his family lived. I judged camp to be straight down below us and about five miles to the northwest through the timber.

The husband was standing, talking to the brother and

gesturing and pointing out that he had seen the sable feeding on the opposite side of the meadow valley and that they must have fed either up or down the valley. We sat in the shelter of the trees and sent the Wander-obo-Masai down into the valley to look for tracks. He came back and reported there were no tracks leading down the valley below us and to the westward, so we knew they had fed on up the meadow valley.

Now the problem was to so use the terrain that we might locate them, and get up and into range of them without being seen. The sun was coming over the hills at the head of the valley and shone on us while every-thing at the head of the valley was in heavy shadow. I told the outfit to stay where they were in the woods, ex-cept for M'Cola and the husband who would go with me, we keeping in the timber and grading up our side of the valley until we could be above and see into the pocket of the curve at the upper end to glass it for the sable.

You ask how this was discussed, worked out, and understood with the bar of language, and I say it was as freely discussed and clearly understood as though we were a cavalry patrol all speaking the same language. We were all hunters except, possibly, Garrick, and the whole thing could be worked out, understood, and agreed to without using anything but a forefinger to signal and a hand to caution. We left them and worked very care-fully ahead, well back in the timber to get height. Then, when we were far enough up and along, we crawled out onto a rocky place and, being behind rock, shielding the glasses with my hat so they would not reflect the sun, M'Cola nodding and grunting as he saw the practicability of that, we glassed the opposite side of the meadow around the edge of the timber, and up into the pocket at the head of the valley; and there they were. M'Cola saw them just before I did and pulled my sleeve.

"N'Dio," I said. Then held my breath to watch them. All looked very black, big necked, and heavy. All had the back-curving horns. They were a long way away. Some were lying down. One was standing. We could see seven.

"Where's the bull?" I whispered.

M'Cola motioned with his left hand and counted four fingers. It was one of those lying down in the tall grass and the animal did look much bigger and the horns much more sweeping. But we were looking into the morning sun and it was hard to see well. Behind them a sort of gully ran up into the hill that blocked the end of the valley.

Now we knew what we had to do. We must go back, cross the meadow far enough down so we were out of sight, get into the timber on the far side and work along through the timber to get above the sable. First we must try to make sure there were no more of them in the timber or the meadow that we must work through before we made our stalk.

I wet my finger and put it up. From the cool side it seemed as though the breeze came down the valley.

M'Cola took some dead leaves and crumpled them and tossed them up. They fell a little toward us. The wind was all right and now we must glass the edge of the timber and check on it.

"Hapana," M'Cola said finally. I had seen nothing either and my eyes ached from the pull of the eight-power glasses. We could take a chance on the timber. We might jump something and spook the sable but we had to take that chance to get around and above them.

We made our way back and down and told the others. From where they were we could cross the valley out of sight of its upper end and bending low, me with my hat off, we headed down into the high meadow grass and across the deeply cut watercourse that ran down through the center of the meadow, across its rocky shelf, and up the grassy bank on the other side, keeping under the edge of a fold of the valley into the shelter of the woods. Then we headed up through the woods, crouched, in single file, to try to get above the sable.

We went forward making as good time as we could and still move quietly. I had made too many stalks on big horn sheep only to find them fed away and out of sight when you came round the shoulder of the mountain to trust these sable to stay where they were and, since once we were in the timber we could no longer see them, I thought it was important that we come up above them as fast as we could without getting me too blown and shaky for the shooting.

M'Cola's water bottle made a noise against the cartridges in his pocket and I stopped and had him pass it to the Wanderobo-Masai. It seemed too many people to be hunting with, but they all moved quietly as snakes, and I was over-confident anyway. I was sure the sable could not see us in the forest, nor wind us.

Finally I was certain we were above them and that they must be ahead of us, and past where the sun was shining in a thinning of the forest, and below us, under the edge of the hill. I checked on the aperture in the sight being clean, cleaned my glasses and wiped the sweat from my forehead remembering to put the used handkerchief in my left pocket so I would not fog my glasses wiping them with it again. M'Cola and I and the husband started to work our way to the edge of the timber; finally crawling almost to the edge of the ridge. There were still some trees between us and the open meadow below and we were behind a small bush and a fallen tree when, raising our heads, we could see them in the grassy open, about three hundred yards away, showing big and very dark in the shadow. Between us was scattered open timber full of sunlight and the openness of the gulch. As we watched two got to their feet and seemed to be standing looking at us. The shot was possible but it was too bloody long to be certain and as I lay, watching, I felt somebody touch me on the arm and Garrick, who had crawled up, whispered throatily, "Piga! Piga, B'wana! Doumi! Doumi!" saying to shoot, that it was a bull. I glanced back and there were the whole outfit on their bellies or hands and knees, the Wanderobo-Masai shaking like a bird dog. I was furious and motioned them all down.

So that was a bull, eh, well there was a much bigger bull that M'Cola and I had seen lying down. The two sable were watching us and I dropped my head, I thought they might be getting a flash from my glasses. When I looked up again, very slowly, I shaded my eyes with my hand. The two sable had stopped looking and were feeding. But one looked up again nervously and I saw the dark, heavy-built antelope with scimitar-like horns swung back staring at us.

I had never seen a sable. I knew nothing about them, neither whether their eyesight was keen, like a ram who sees you at whatever distance you see him, or like a bull elk who cannot see you at two hundred yards unless you move. I was not sure of their size either, but I judged the range to be all of three hundred yards. I knew I could hit one if I shot from a sitting position or prone, but I could not say where I would hit him.

Then Garrick again, "Piga B'wana Piga!" I turned on him as though to slug him in the mouth. It would have been a great comfort to do it. I truly was not nervous when I first saw the sable, but Garrick was making me nervous.

"Far," I whispered to M'Cola who had crawled up and was lying by me.

"Yes."

"Shoot?"

"No. Glasses."

We both watched, using the glasses guardedly. I could only see four. There had been seven. If that was a bull that Garrick pointed out, then they were all bulls. They all looked the same color in the shadow. Their horns all looked big to me. I knew that with mountain sheep the rams all kept together in bunches until late in the winter when they went with the ewes; that in the late summer you found bull elk in bunches too, before the rutting season, and that later they herded up together again. We had seen as many as twenty impalla rams together up on the Serenea. All right, then, they could all be bulls, but I wanted a good one, the best one, and I tried to remember having read something about them, but all I could remember was a silly story of some man seeing the same bull every morning in the same place and never getting up on him. All I could remember was the wonderful pair of horns we had seen in the Game Warden's office in Arusha. And here were sable now, and I must play it right and get the best one. It never occurred to me that Garrick had never seen a sable and that he knew no more about them than M'Cola or I.

"Too far," I said to M'Cola.

"Yes."

"Come on," I said, then waved the others down, and we started crawling up to reach the edge of the hill.

Finally we lay behind a tree and I looked around it.

Now we could see their horns clearly with the glasses and could see the other three. One, lying down, was certainly much the biggest and the horns, as I caught them in silhouette, seemed to curve much higher and farther back. I was studying them, too excited to be happy as I watched them, when I heard M'Cola whisper "B'wana."

I lowered the glasses and looked and there was Garrick, taking no advantage of the cover, crawling on his hands and knees out to join us. I put my hand out, palm toward him, and waved him down but he paid no attention and came crawling on, as conspicuous as a man walking down a city street on hands and knees. I saw one sable looking toward us, toward him, rather. Then three more got to their feet. Then the big one got up and stood broadside with head turned toward us as Garrick came up whispering, "Piga, B'wana! Piga! Doumi! Doumi! Kubwa Sana."

There was no choice now. They were definitely spooked and I lay out flat on my belly, put my arm through the sling, got my elbows settled and my right toe pushing the ground and squeezed off on the center of the bull's shoulder. But at the roar I knew it was bad. I was over him. They all jumped and stood looking, not knowing where the noise came from. I shot again at the bull and threw dirt all over him and they were off. I was on my feet and hit him as he ran and he was down. Then he was up and I hit him again and he took it and was in the bunch. They passed him and I shot and was behind him. Then I hit him again and he was trailing slowly and I knew I had him. M'Cola was handing me cartridges and I was shoving shells down into the damned-to-hell, lousy, staggered, Springfield magazine watching the sable making heavy weather of it crossing the watercourse. We had him all right. I could see he was very sick. The others were trailing up into the timber. In the sunlight on the other side they looked much lighter and the one I'd shot looked lighter, too. They looked a dark chestnut and the one I had shot was almost black. But he was not black and I felt there was something wrong. I shoved the last shell in and Garrick was trying to grab my hand to congratulate me when, below us across the open space where the gully that we could not see opened onto the head of the valley, sable started to pass at a running stampede.

"Good God," I thought. They all looked like the one I had shot and I was trying to pick a big one. They all looked about the same and they were crowding running and then came the bull. Even in the shadow he was a dead black and shiny as he hit the sun, and his horns swept up high, then back, huge and dark, in two great curves nearly touching the middle of his back. He was a bull all right. God, what a bull.

"Doumi," said M'Cola in my ear. "Doumi!"

I hit him and at the roar he was down. I saw him up, the others passing, spreading out, then bunching. I missed him. Then I saw him going almost straight away up the valley in the tall grass and I hit him again and he went out of sight. The sable now were going up the hill at the head of the valley, up the hill at our right, up the hill in the timber across the valley, spread out and travelling fast. Now that I had seen a bull I knew they all were cows including the first one I had shot. The bull never showed and I was absolutely sure that we would find him where I had seen him go down in the long grass.

The outfit were all up and I shook off handshaking and thumb pulling before we started down through the trees and over the edge of the gully and to the meadow on a dead run. My eyes, my mind, and all inside of me were full of the blackness of that sable bull and the sweep of those horns and I was thanking God I had the rifle reloaded before he came out. But it was excited shooting, all of it, and I was not proud of it. I had gotten excited and shot at the whole animal instead of the right place and I was ashamed; but the outfit now were drunk excited. I would have walked but you could not hold them, they were like a pack of dogs as we ran. As we crossed the meadow opening where we had first seen the seven and went beyond where the bull had gone out of sight, the grass suddenly was high and over our heads and every one slowed down. There were two washed-out concealed ravines ten or twelve feet deep that ran down to the watercourse and what had looked a smooth grass-filled basin was very broken, tricky country with grass that was from waist-high to well above our heads. We found blood at once and it led off to the left, across the watercourse and up the hillside on the left toward the head of the valley. I thought that was the first sable but it seemed a wider swing than he had seemed to make when we watched him going from above in the timber. I made a circle to look for the big bull but I could not pick his track from the mass of tracks and in the high grass and the broken terrain it was difficult to figure just where he had gone.

They were all for the blood spoor and it was like trying to make badly-trained bird dogs hunt a dead bird when they are crazy to be off after the rest of the covey.

"Doumi! Doumi!" I said. "Kubwa Sana! The bull. The big bull."

"Yes," everybody agreed. "Here! Here!" The blood spoor that crossed the watercourse.

Finally I took that trail thinking we must get them one at a time, and knowing this one was hard hit and the other would keep. Then, too, I might be wrong and this might be the big bull, he might possibly have turned in the high grass and crossed here as we were running down. I had been wrong before, I remembered.

We trailed fast up the hillside, into the timber, the blood was splashed freely; made a turn toward the right, climbing steeply, and at the head of the valley in some large rocks jumped a sable. It went scrambling and bounding off through the rocks. I saw in an instant that it was not hit and knew that, in spite of the back-swung dark horns, it was a cow from the dark chestnut color. But I saw this just in time to keep from shooting. I had started to pull when I lowered the rifle.

"Manamouki," I said. "It's a cow."

M'Cola and the two Roman guides agreed. I had very nearly shot. We went on perhaps five yards and another sable jumped. But this one was swaying its head wildly and could not clear the rocks. It was hard hit and I took my time, shot carefully, and broke its neck.

We came up to it, lying in the rocks, a large, deep chestnut-brown animal, almost black, the horns black and curving handsomely back, there was a white patch on the muzzle and back from the eye, there was a white belly; but it was no bull.

M'Cola, still in doubt, verified this and feeling of the short, rudimentary teats said "Manamouki," and shook his head sadly.

It was the first big bull that Garrick had pointed out.

"Bull down there," I pointed.

"Yes," said M'Cola.

I thought that we would give him time to get sick, if he were only wounded, and then go down and find him. So I had M'Cola make the cuts for taking off the head skin and we would leave the old man to skin out the head while we went down after the bull.

I drank some water from the canteen. I was thirsty after the run and the climb and the sun was up now and it was getting hot. Then we went down the opposite side of the valley from that we had just come up trailing the wounded cow, and below, in the tall grass, casting in circles, commenced to hunt for the trail of the bull. We could not find it.

The sable had been running in a bunch as they came out and any individual track was confused or obliterated. We found some blood on the grass stems where I had first hit him, then lost it, then found it again where the other blood spoor turned off. Then the tracks had all split up as they had gone, fan-wise, up the valley and the hills and we could not find it again. Finally I found blood on a grass blade about fifty yards up the valley and I plucked it and held it up. This was a mistake. I should have brought them to it. Already every one but M'Cola was losing faith in the bull.

He was not there. He had disappeared. He had vanished. Perhaps he had never existed. Who could say he was a real bull? If I had not plucked the grass with the blood on it I might have held them. Growing there with blood on it, it was evidence. Plucked, it meant nothing except to me and to M'Cola. But I could find no more blood and they were all hunting half-heartedly now. The only possible way was to quarter every foot of the high grass and trace every foot of the gullies. It was very hot now and they were only making a pretense of hunting.

Garrick came up. "All cows," he said. "No bull. Just biggest cow. You killed biggest cow. We found her. Smaller cow get away."

"You wind-blown son of a bitch," I said, then, using my fingers. "Listen. Seven cows. Then fifteen cows and one bull. Bull hit. Here."

"All cows," said Garrick.

"One big cow hit. One bull hit."

I was so sure sounding that they agreed to this and searched for a while but I could see they were losing belief in the bull.

"If I had one good dog," I thought. "Just one good dog."

Then Garrick came up. "All cows," he said. "Very big cows."

"You're a cow," I said. "Very big cow."

This got a laugh from the Wanderobo-Masai, who was getting to look a picture of sick misery. The brother half believed in the bull, I could see. Husband, by now, did not believe in any of us. I didn't think he even believed in the kudu of the night before. Well, after this shooting, I did not blame him.

M'Cola came up. "Hapana," he said glumly. Then, "B'wana, you shot that bull?"

"Yes," I said. For a minute I began to doubt whether there ever was a bull. Then I saw again his heavy, high-withered blackness and the high rise of his horns before they swept back, him running with the bunch, shoulder higher than them and black as hell and as I saw it, M'Cola saw it again too through the rising mist of the savage's unbelief in what he can no longer see.

263

"Yes," M'Cola agreed. "I see him. You shoot him."

I told it again. "Seven cows. Shoot biggest. Fifteen cows, one bull. Hit that bull."

They all believed it now for a moment and circled, searching, but the faith died at once in the heat of the sun and the tall grass blowing.

"All cows," Garrick said. The Wanderobo-Masai nodded, his mouth open. I could feel the comfortable lack of faith coming over me too. It was a damned sight easier not to hunt in that sun in that shadeless pocket and in the sun on that steep hillside. I told M'Cola we would hunt up the valley on both sides, finish skinning out the head, and he and I would come down alone and find the bull. You could not hunt them against that unbelief. I had had no chance to train them; no power to discipline. If there had been no law I would have shot Garrick and they would all have hunted or cleared out. I think they would have hunted. Garrick was not popular. He was simply poison.

M'Cola and I came back down the valley, quartered it like bird dogs, circled and followed and checked track after track. I was hot and very thirsty. The sun was something serious by now.

"Hapana," M'Cola said. We could not find him. Whatever he was, we had lost him.

"Maybe he was a cow. Maybe it was all goofy," I thought, letting the unbelief come in as a comfort. We were going to hunt up the side hill to the right and then we would have checked it all and would take the cow head into camp and see what the Roman had located. I was dead thirsty and drained the canteen. We would get water in camp.

We started up the hill and I jumped a sable in some brush. I almost loosed off at it before I saw it was a cow. That showed how one could be hidden, I thought. We would have to get the men and go over it all again; and then, from the old man, came a wild shouting.

"Doumi! Doumi!" in a high, screaming shout.

"Where?" I shouted, running across the hill toward him.

"There! There!" he shouted, pointing into the timber on the other side of the head of the valley. "There! There! There he goes! There!"

We came on a dead run but the bull was out of sight in the timber on the hillside. The old man said he was huge, he was black, he had great horns, and he came by him ten yards away, hit in two places, in the gut and high up in the rump, hard hit but going fast, crossing the valley, through the boulders and going up the hillside.

I gut-shot him, I thought. Then as he was going away I laid that one on his stern. He lay down and was sick and we missed him. Then, when we were past, he jumped.

"Come on," I said. Every one was excited and ready to go now and the old man was chattering about the bull as he folded the head skin and put the head up on his own head and we started across through the rocks and up, quartering up onto the hillside. There, where the old man had pointed, was a very big sable track, the hoof marks spread wide, the tracks grading up into the timber and there was blood, plenty of it.

We trailed him fast, hoping to jump him and have a shot, and it was easy trailing in the shade of the trees with plenty of blood to follow. But he kept climbing, grading up around the hill, and he was travelling fast. We kept the blood bright and wet but we could not come up on him. I did not track but kept watching ahead thinking I might see him as he looked back, or see him down, or cutting down across the hill through the timber, and M'Cola and Garrick were tracking, aided by every one but the old man who staggered along with the sable skull and head skin held on his own gray head. M'Cola had hung the empty water bottle on him, and Garrick had loaded him with the cinema camera. It was hard going for the old man.

Once we came on a place where the bull had rested and watched his back track, there was a little pool of blood on a rock where he had stood, behind some bushes, and I cursed the wind that blew our scent on ahead of us. There was a big breeze blowing now and I was certain we had no chance of surprising him, our scent would keep everything moving out of the way ahead of us as long as anything could move. I thought of trying to circle ahead with M'Cola and let them track but we were moving fast, the blood was still bright on the stones and on the fallen leaves and grass and the hills were too steep for us to make a circle. I did not see how we could lose him.

Then he took us up and into a rocky, ravine-cut country where the trailing was slow and the climbing difficult. Here, I thought, we would jump him in a gully but the spatters of blood, not so bright now, went on around the boulders, over the rocks and up and up and left us on a rim-rock ledge. He must have gone down from there. It was too steep above for him to have gone over the top of the hill. There was no other way to go but down, but how had he gone, and down which ravine? I sent them looking down three possible ways and got out on the rim to try to sight him. They could not find any spoor, and then the Wanderobo-Masai called from below and to the right that he had blood and, climbing down, we saw it on a rock and then followed it in occasional drying splatters down through a steep descent to the meadow below. I was encouraged when he started down hill and in the knee-high, heavy grass of the meadow trailing was easy again, because the grass brushed against his belly and while you could not see tracks clearly without stooping double and parting the grass to look, yet the blood spoor was plain on the grass blades. But it was dry now and dully shiny and I knew we had lost much time on him when he rim-rocked us on the hill.

Finally his trail crossed the dry watercourse about

where we had first come in sight of the meadow in the morning and led away into the sloping, sparsely-wooded country on the far side. There were no clouds and I could feel the sun now, not just as heat but as a heavy deadly weight on my head and I was very thirsty. It was very hot but it was not the heat that bothered. It was the weight of the sun.

Garrick had given up tracking seriously and was only contributing theatrical successes of discovering blood when M'Cola and I were checked. He would do no routine tracking any more, but would rest and then track in irritating spurts. The Wanderobo-Masai was useless as a blue-jay and I had M'Cola give him the big rifle to carry so that we would get some use out of him. The Roman's brother was obviously not a hunter and the husband was not very interested. He did not seem to be a hunter either. As we trailed, slowly, the ground, hard now as the sun had baked it, the blood only black spots and splatters on the short grass, one by one the brother, Garrick, and the Wanderobo-Masai dropped out and sat in the shade of the scattered trees.

The sun was terrific and as it was necessary to track with heads bent down and stooping, in spite of a handkerchief spread over my neck I had a pounding ache in my head.

M'Cola was tracking slowly, steadily, and absolutely absorbed in the problem. His bare, bald head gleamed with sweat and when it ran down in his eyes he would pluck a grass stem, hold it with each hand and shave the sweat off his forehead and bald black crown with the stem.

We went on slowly. I had always sworn to Pop that I could out-track M'Cola but I realized now that in the past I had been giving a sort of Garrick performance in picking up the spoor when it was lost and that in straight, steady trailing, now in the heat, with the sun really bad, truly bad so that you could feel what it was doing to your head, cooking it to hell, trailing in short grass on hard ground where a blood spot was a dry, black blister on a grass blade, difficult to see; that you must find the next little black spot perhaps twenty yards away, one holding the last blood while the other found the next, then going on, one on each side of the trail; pointing with a grass stem at the spots to save talking, until it ran out again and you marked the last blood with your eye and both made casts to pick it up again, signalling with a hand up, my mouth too dry to talk, a heat shimmer over the ground now when you straightened up to let your neck stop aching and looked ahead, I knew M'Cola was immeasurably the better man and the better tracker. Have to tell Pop, I thought.

At this point M'Cola made a joke. My mouth was so dry that it was hard to talk.

"B'wana," M'Cola said, looking at me when I had straightened up and was leaning my neck back to get the crick out of it.

"Yes?"

"Whiskey?" and he offered me the flask.

"You bastard," I said in English and he chuckled and shook his head.

"Hapana whiskey?"

"You savage," I said in Swahili.

We started tracking again, M'Cola shaking his head and very amused, and in a little while the grass was longer and it was easier again. We crossed all that semi-open country we had seen from the hillside in the morning and going down a slope the tracks swung back into high grass. In this higher grass I found that by half shutting my eyes I could see his trail where he had shouldered through the grass and I went ahead fast without trailing by the blood, to M'Cola's amazement, but then we came out on very short grass and rock again and now the trailing was the hardest yet.

He was not bleeding much now; the sun and the heat must have dried the wounds and we found only an occasional small starry splatter on the rocky ground.

Garrick came up and made a couple of brilliant discoveries of blood spots, then sat down under a tree. Under another tree I could see the poor old Wanderobo-Masai holding his first and last job as gun bearer. Under another was the old man, the sable head beside him like some black-mass symbol, his equipment hanging from his shoulders. M'Cola and I went on trailing very slowly and laboriously across the long stony slope and back and up into another tree-scattered meadow, and through it, and into a long field with piled up boulders at the end. In the middle of this field we lost the trail completely and circled and hunted for nearly two hours before we found blood again.

The old man found it for us below the boulders and to the right a half a mile away. He had gone ahead down there on his own idea of what the bull would have done. The old man was a hunter.

Then we trailed him very slowly, onto hard stony ground a mile away. But we could not trail from there. The ground was too hard to leave a track and we never found blood again. Then we hunted on our various theories of where the bull would go, but the country was too big and we had no luck.

"No good," M'Cola said.

I straightened up and went over to the shade of a big tree. It felt cool as water and the breeze cooled my skin through the wet shirt. I was thinking about the bull and wishing to God I had never hit him. Now I had wounded him and lost him. I believe he kept right on travelling and went out of that country. He never showed any tendency to circle back. Tonight he would die and the hyenas would eat him, or, worse, they would get him before he died, hamstringing him and pulling his guts out while he was alive. The first one that hit that blood spoor would stay with it until he found him. Then he would call up the others. I felt a son of a bitch to have

hit him and not killed him. I did not mind killing anything, any animal, if I killed it cleanly, they all had to
die and my interference with the nightly and the seasonal
killing that went on all the time was very minute and
I had no guilty feeling at all. We ate the meat and kept
the hides and horns. But I felt rotten sick over this sable
bull. Besides, I wanted him. I wanted him damned badly,
I wanted him more than I would admit. Well, we had
played our string out with him. Our chance was at the
start when he was down and we missed him. We had
lost that. No, our best chance, the only chance a rifle-
man should ever ask, was when I had a shot and shot at
the whole animal instead of calling the shot. It was my
own lousy fault. I was a son of a bitch to have gut-shot
him. It came from over-confidence in being able to do
a thing and then omitting one of the steps in how it is
done. Well, we had lost him. I doubted if there was
a dog in the world could trail him now in that heat. Still
that was the only chance. I got out the dictionary and
asked the old man if there were any dogs at the Roman's
place.

"No," said the old man. "Hapana."

We made a very wide circle and I sent the brother and
the husband out in another circle. We found nothing,
no trace, no tracks, no blood, and I told M'Cola we would
start for camp. The Roman's brother and the husband
went up the valley to get the meat of the sable cow
we had shot. We were beaten.

M'Cola and I ahead, the others following, we went across the long heat haze of the open country, down to cross the dry watercourse, and up and into the grateful shade of the trail through the woods. As we were going along through the broken sunlight and shadow, the floor of the forest smooth and springy where we cut across to save distance from the trail, we saw, less than a hundred yards away, a herd of sable standing in the timber looking at us. I pulled back the bolt and looked for the best pair of horns.

"Doumi," Garrick whispered. "Doumi kubwa sana!"

I looked where he pointed. It was a very big cow sable, dark chestnut, white marks on the face, white belly, heavy built and with a fine curving pair of horns. She was standing broadside to us with her head turned, looking. I looked carefully at the whole lot. They were all cows; evidently the bunch whose bull I had wounded and lost, and they had come over the hill and herded up again together here.

"We go to camp," I said to M'Cola.

As we started forward the sable jumped and ran past us, crossing the trail ahead. At every good pair of cow horns Garrick said, "Bull, B'wana. Big, big bull. Shoot, B'wana. Shoot, oh, shoot!"

"All cows," I said to M'Cola when they were past, running in a panic through the sun-splashed timber.

"Yes," he agreed.

"Old man," I said. The old man came up.

"Let the guide carry that," I said.

The old man lowered the cow sable head.

"No," said Garrick.

"Yes," I said. "Bloody well yes."

We went on through the woods toward camp. I was feeling better, much better. All through the day I had never thought once of the kudu. Now we were coming home to where they were waiting.

It seemed much longer coming home although, usually, the return over a new trail is shorter. I was tired all the way into my bones, my head felt cooked, and I was thirstier than I had ever been in my life. But suddenly, walking through the woods, it was much cooler. A cloud had come over the sun.

We came out of the timber and down onto the flat and in sight of the thorn fence. The sun was behind a bank of clouds now and then in a little while the sky was covered completely and the clouds looked heavy and threatening. I thought perhaps this had been the last clear hot day; unusual heat before the rains. First I thought: if it had only rained, so that the ground would hold a track, we could have stayed with that bull forever; then, looking at the heavy, woolly clouds that so quickly had covered all the sky, I thought that if we were going to join the outfit, and get the car across that ten-mile stretch of black cotton road on the way to Handeni, we had better start. I pointed to the sky.

"Bad," M'Cola agreed.

"Go to the camp of B'wana M'Kubwa?"

"Better." Then, vigorously, accepting the decision, "N'Dio. N'Dio."

"We go," I said.

Arrived at the thorn fence and the hut, we broke camp fast. There was a runner there from our last camp who had brought a note, written before P. O. M. and Pop had left, and bringing my mosquito net. There was nothing in the note, only good luck and that they were starting. I drank some water from one of our canvas bags, sat on a petrol tin and looked at the sky. I could not, conscientiously, chance staying. If it rained here we might not even be able to get out to the road. If it rained heavily on the road, we would never get out to the coast that season. Both the Austrian and Pop had said that. I had to go.

That was settled so there was no use to think how much I wanted to stay. The day's fatigue helped make the decision easy. Everything was being loaded into the car and they were all gathering up their meat from the sticks around the ashes of the fire.

"Don't you want to eat, B'wana?" Kamau asked me.

"No," I said. Then in English, "Too bloody tired."

"Eat. You are hungry."

"Later, in the car."

M'Cola went by with a load, his big, flat face completely blank again. It only came alive about hunting or some joke. I found a tin cup by the fire and called to him to bring the whiskey, and the blank face cracked at the eyes and mouth into a smile as he took the flask out of his pocket.

"With water better," he said.

"You black Chinaman."

They were all working fast and the Roman's women came over and stood a little way away watching the carrying and the packing of the car. There were two of them, good-looking, well built, and shy, but interested. The Roman was not back yet. I felt very badly to go off like this with no explanation to him. I liked the Roman very much and had a high regard for him.

I took a drink of the whiskey and water and looked at the two pairs of kudu horns that leaned against the wall of the chicken coop hut. From the white, cleanly picked skulls the horns rose in slow spirals that spreading made a turn, another turn, and then curved delicately in to those smooth, ivory-like points. One pair was narrower and taller against the side of the hut. The other was almost as tall but wider in spread and heavier in beam. They were the color of black walnut meats and they were beautiful to see. I went over and stood the Springfield against the hut between them and the tips reached past the muzzle of the rifle. As Kamau came back from carrying a load to the car I told him to bring the camera and then had him stand beside them while I took a picture. Then he picked them up, each head a load, and carried them over to the car.

Garrick was talking loudly and in a roostery way to the Roman's women. As near as I could make out he was offering them the empty petrol boxes in exchange for a piece of something.

"Come here," I called to him. He came over still feeling smart.

"Listen," I told him in English. "If I get through this safari without socking you it's going to be a bloody marvel. And if I ever hit you I'll break your mucking jaw. That's all."

He did not understand the words but the tone made it clearer than if I had gotten something out of the dictionary to tell him. I stood up and motioned to the women that they could have the petrol tins and the cases. I was damned if I could not have anything to do with them if I would let Garrick make any passes.

"Get in the car," I told him. "No," as he started to make delivery of one of the petrol tins, "in the car." He went over to the car.

We were all packed now and ready to go. The horns were curling out the back of the car, tied onto the loads. I left some money for the Roman and one of the kudu hides with the boy. Then we got in the car. I got in the front seat with the Wanderobo-Masai. In back were M'Cola, Garrick, and the runner, who was a man from the old man's village by the road. The old man was crouched on top of the loads in back, close under the roof.

We waved and started, passing more of the Roman's household, the older and uglier part, roasting up piles of meat by a log fire beside the trail that came up from the river through the maize field. We made the crossing all right, the creek was down and the banks had dried and I looked back at the field, the Roman's huts, and the stockade where we had camped, and the blue hills, dark under the heavy sky, and I felt very badly not to have seen the Roman and explain why we had gone off like this.

Then we were going through the woods, following our trail and trying to make time to get out before dark. We had trouble, twice, at boggy places and Garrick seemed to be in a state of great hysteria, ordering people about when we were cutting brush and shovelling until I was certain I would have to hit him. He called for corporal punishment the way a showing-off child does for a spanking. Kamau and M'Cola were both laughing at him. He was playing the victorious leader home from the chase now. I thought it was really a shame that he could not have his ostrich plumes.

Once when we were stuck and I was shovelling and he was stooping over in a frenzy of advice and command-giving, I brought the handle of the shovel, with manifest un-intention, up hard into his belly, and he sat down backwards. I never looked toward him, and M'Cola, Kamau, and I could not look at each other for fear we would laugh.

"I am hurt," he said in astonishment, getting to his feet.

"Never get near a man shovelling," I said in English. "Damned dangerous."

"I am hurt," said Garrick holding his belly.

"Rub it," I told him and rubbed mine to show him how. We all got in the car again and I began to feel sorry for the poor, bloody, useless, theatrical bastard, so I told M'Cola I would drink a bottle of beer. He got one out from under the loads in back, we were going through the deer-park-looking country now, opened it, and I drank it slowly. I looked around and saw Garrick was all right now, letting his mouth run freely again. He rubbed his belly and seemed to be telling them what a hell of a man he was and how he had never felt it. I could feel the old man watching me from up under the roof as I drank the beer.

"Old man," I said.

"Yes, B'wana."

"A present," and I handed what was left in the bottle back. There wasn't much left but the foam and a very little beer.

"Beer?" asked M'Cola.

"By God, yes," I said. I was thinking about beer and in my mind was back to that year in the spring when we walked on the mountain road to the Bains de Alliez and the beer-drinking contest where we failed to win the calf and came home that night around the mountain with the moonlight on the fields of narcissus that grew on the meadows and how we were drunk and talked about how you would describe that light on that paleness, and the brown beer sitting at the wood tables under the wisteria vine at Aigle when we came in across the Rhone Valley from fishing the Stockalper with the horse chestnut trees in bloom and Chink and I again discussing writing and whether you could call them waxen candelabras. God, what bloody literary discussions we had; we were literary as hell then just after the war, and later there was the good beer at Lipp's at midnight after Mascart-Ledoux at the Cirque de Paris or Routis-Ledoux, or after any other great fight where you lost your voice and were still too exicted to turn in; but beer was mostly those years just after the war with Chink and in the mountains. Flags for the Fusilier, crags for the Mountaineer, for English poets beer, strong beer for me. That was Chink then, quoting Robert Graves, then. We outgrew some countries and we went to others but beer was still a bloody marvel. The old man knew it too. I had seen it in his eye the first time he saw me take a drink.

"Beer," said M'Cola. He had it open, and I looked out at that park-like country, the engine hot under my boots, the Wanderobo-Masai as strong as ever beside me, Kamau watching the grooves of the tire tracks in the green turf, and I hung my booted legs over the side to let my feet cool and drank the beer and wished old Chink was along. Captain Eric Edward Dorman-Smith, M.C.

of His Majesty's Fifth Fusiliers. Now if he were there we could discuss how to describe this deer park country and whether deer park was enough to call it. Pop and Chink were much alike. Pop was older and more tolerant for his years and the same sort of company. I was learning under Pop, while Chink and I had discovered a big part of the world together and then our ways had gone a long way apart.

But that damned sable bull. I should have killed him; but it was a running shot. To hit him at all I had to use him all as a target. Yes, you bastard, but what about the cow you missed twice, prone, standing broadside? Was that a running shot? No. If I'd gone to bed last night I would not have done that. Or if I'd wiped out the bore to get the oil out she would not have thrown high the first time. Then I would not have pulled down and shot under her the second shot. Every damned thing is your own fault if you're any good. I thought I could shoot a shot-gun better than I could and I had lost plenty of money backing my opinion but I knew, coldly and outside myself, that I could shoot a rifle on game as well as any son of a bitch that ever lived. Like hell I could. So what? So I gut-shot a sable bull and let him get away. Could I shoot as well as I thought I could? Sure. Then why did I miss on that cow? Hell, everybody is off sometime. You've got no bloody business to be off. Who the hell are you? My conscience? Listen, I'm all right with my conscience. I know just what kind of a son of a bitch I am and I know what I can do well. If I hadn't had to leave and pull out I would have got a sable bull. You know the Roman was a hunter. There was another herd. Why did I have to make a one night stand? Was that any way to hunt? Hell, no. I'd make some money some way and when we came back we would come to the old man's village in trucks, then pack in with porters so there wouldn't be any damned car to worry about, send the porters back, and make a camp in the timber up the stream above the Roman's and hunt that country slowly, living there and hunting out each day, sometimes laying off and writing for a week, or writing half the day, or every other day, and get to know it as I knew the country around the lake where we were brought up. I'd see the buffalo feeding where they lived, and when the elephants came through the hills we would see them and watch them breaking branches and not have to shoot, and I would lie in the fallen leaves and watch the kudu feed out and never fire a shot unless I saw a better head than this one in back, and instead of trailing that sable bull, gut-shot to hell, all day, I'd lie behind a rock and watch them on the hillside and see them long enough so they belonged to me forever. Sure, if Garrick didn't take his B'wana Simba back in there and shoot the country out. But if he did I'd go on down beyond those hills and there would be another country where a man could live and hunt if he had time to live and hunt. They'd gone in wherever a car could go. But there must be pockets like this all over, that no one knows of, that the cars pass all along the road. They all hunt the same places.

"Beer?" asked M'Cola.

"Yes," I said.

Sure, you couldn't make a living. Every one had explained that. The locusts came and ate your crops and the monsoon failed, and the rains did not come, and everything dried up and died. There were ticks and fly to kill the stock, and the mosquitoes gave you fever and maybe you got blackwater. Your cattle would die and you would get no price for your coffee. It took an Indian to make money from sisal and on the coast every cocoanut plantation meant a man ruined by the idea or making money from copra. A white hunter worked three months out of the year and drank for twelve and the Government was ruining the country for the benefit of the Hindu and the natives. That was what they told you. Sure. But I did not want to make money. All I wanted was to live in it and have time to hunt. Already I had had one of the diseases and had experienced the necessity of washing a three-inch bit of my large intestine with soap and water and tucking it back where it belonged an unnumbered amount of times a day. There were remedies which cured this and it was well worth going through for what I had seen and where I had been. Besides I caught that on the dirty boat out from Marseilles. P. O. M. hadn't been ill a day. Neither had Karl. I loved this country and I felt at home and where a man feels at home, outside of where he's born, is where he's meant to go. Then, in my grandfather's time, Michigan was a malaria ridden state. They called it fever and ague. And in Tortugas, where I'd spent months, a thousand men once died of yellow fever. New continents and islands try to frighten you with disease as a snake hisses. The snake may be poisonous too. You kill them off. Hell, what I had a month ago would have killed me in the old days before they invented the remedies. Maybe it would and maybe I would have gotten well.

It is easier to keep well in a good country by taking simple precautions than to pretend that a country which is finished is still good.

A continent ages quickly once we come. The natives live in harmony with it. But the foreigner destroys, cuts down the trees, drains the water, so that the water supply is altered and in a short time the soil, once the sod is turned under, is cropped out and, next, it starts to blow away as it has blown away in every old country and as I had seen it start to blow in Canada. The earth gets tired of being exploited. A country wears out quickly unless man puts back in it all his residue and that of all his beasts. When he quits using beasts and uses machines, the earth defeats him quickly. The machine can't reproduce, nor does it fertilize the soil, and it eats what he cannot raise. A country was made to be as we found it. We are the intruders and after we are dead we may have ruined it but it will still be there and we don't know what the next changes are. I suppose they all end up like Mongolia.

I would come back to Africa but not to make a living from it. I could do that with two pencils and a few hundred sheets of the cheapest paper. But I would come back to where it pleased me to live; to really live. Not just let my life pass. Our people went to America because that was the place to go then. It had been a good country and we had made a bloody mess of it and I would go, now, somewhere else as we had always had the right to go somewhere else and as we had always gone. You could always come back. Let the others come to America who did not know that they had come too late. Our people had seen it at its best and fought for it when it was well worth fighting for. Now I would go somewhere else. We always went in the old days and there were still good places to go.

I knew a good country when I saw one. Here there was game, plenty of birds, and I liked the natives. Here I could shoot and fish. That, and writing, and reading, and seeing pictures was all I cared about doing. And I could remember all the pictures. Other things I liked to watch but they were what I liked to do. That and ski-ing. But my legs were bad now and it was not worth the time you spent hunting good snow any more. You saw too many people, ski-ing now.

Now, the car making a turn around a bank and crossing a green, grassy field, we came in sight of the Masai village.

When the Masai saw us they started running out and we stopped, surrounded by them, just below the stockade. There were the young warriors who had run with us, and now their women and the children all came out to see us. The children were all quite young and the men and women all seemed the same age. There were no old people. They all seemed to be our great friends and we gave a very successful party with refreshments in the shape of our bread which they all ate with much laughing, the men first, then the women. Then I had M'Cola open the two cans of mince meat and the plum pudding and I cut these into rations and passed them out. I had heard and read that the Masai subsisted only on the blood of their cattle mixed with milk, drawing the blood off from a wound in a vein of the neck made by shooting an arrow at close range. These Masai, however, ate bread, cold mince meat, and plum pudding with great relish and much laughter and joking. One very tall and handsome one kept asking me something that I did not understand and then five or six more joined in. Whatever this was they wanted it very badly. Finally the tallest one made a very strange face and emitted a sound like a dying pig. I understood finally; he was asking if we had one of those, and I pressed the button of the klaxon. The children ran screaming, the warriors laughed and laughed, and then as Kamau, in response to popular demand, pressed the klaxon again and again, I watched the look of utter rapture and ecstasy on the women's faces and knew that with that klaxon he could have had any woman in the tribe.

Finally we had to go and after distributing the empty beer bottles, the labels from the bottles, and finally the bottle caps, picked up by M'Cola from the floor, we left, klaxoning the women into ecstasy, the children into panic, and the warriors into delight. The warriors ran with us for a good way but we had to make time, the going was good through the park-like country and, in a little while, we waved to the last of them standing straight and tall, in their brown skin garments, their clubbed pigtails hanging, their faces stained a red-brown, leaning on their spears, looking after us and smiling.

The sun was almost down and as I did not know the road I had the runner get up in front to sit with the Wanderobo-Masai and help direct Kamau and I sat in the back with M'Cola and Garrick. We were out of the park country and onto the dry bush-spattered plain before the sun went down and I had another bottle of the German beer and, watching the country, saw, suddenly, that all the trees were full of white storks. I did not know whether they were there in migration or were following the locusts but, in the twilight, they were lovely to see and, deeply moved by them, I gave the old man a good two fingers of beer that was left in the bottom of the bottle.

On the next bottle I forgot and drank it all before I remembered the old man. (There were still storks in the trees and we saw some Grant's gazelles feeding off to the right. A jackal, like a gray fox, trotted across the road.) So I told M'Cola to open another bottle and we were through the plain and climbing the long slope toward the road and the village, the two mountains in sight now, and it almost dark and quite cold when I handed the bottle to the old man, who took it where he was crouched up under the roof, and nursed it tenderly.

At the village we stopped in the road in the dark, and I paid the runner the amount it said to give him in the note he had brought. I paid the old man the amount Pop said to pay him and a bonus. Then there was a big dispute among them all. Garrick was to go to the main camp to get his money. Abdullah insisted upon going along. He did not trust Garrick. The Wanderobo-Masai insisted pitifully that he go. He was sure the others would cheat him out of his share and I was fairly sure they would, too. There was petrol that had been left for us to use in case we were short and for us to bring in any event. We were overloaded and I did not know how the road was ahead. But I thought we might carry Abdullah and Garrick and squeeze in the Wanderobo-Masai. There was no question of the old man going. He had been paid off and had agreed to the amount, but now he would not leave the car. He crouched on top of the load and hung onto the ropes saying, "I am going with B'wana." 288

M'Cola and Kamau had to break his handholds and pull him off to re-load, him shouting, "I want to go with B'wana!"

While they were loading in the dark he held onto my arm and talked very quietly in a language that I could not understand.

"You have the shillings," I said.

"Yes, B'wana," he said. That was not what it was about. The money was all right.

Then, when we started to get in the car he broke away and started to climb up through the back and onto the loads. Garrick and Abdullah pulled him down.

"You can't go. There isn't room."

He talked to me softly again, begging and pleading.

"No, there is no room."

I remembered I had a small penknife and I got it out of my pocket and put it in his hand. He pushed it back in my hand.

"No," he said. "No."

He was quiet then and stood by the road. But when we started, he started to run after the car and I could hear him in the dark screaming, "B'wana! I want to go with B'wana!"

We went on up the road, the headlights making it seem like a boulevard after where we had been. We drove fifty-five miles on that road in the dark night without incident. I stayed awake until after we were through the bad part, a long plain of deeply rutted black cotton where the headlights picked out the trail through bushes and then, when the road was better, I went to sleep, waking occasionally to see the headlights shining on a wall of tall trees, or a naked bank, or when we ground in low gear up a steep place the light slanting up ahead.

Finally, when the speedometer showed fifty miles, we stopped and woke a native in his hut and M'Cola asked about the camp. I slept again and then woke as we were turning off the road and on a track through trees with the fires of the camp showing ahead. Then as we came to where our lights shone on the green tents I shouted and we all commenced to shout and blew the klaxon and I let the gun off, the flame cutting up into the dark and it making a great noise. Then we were stopped and out from Pop's tent I saw him coming, thick and heavy in his dressing gown, and then he had his arms around my shoulders and said, "You god damned bull fighter," and I was clapping him on the back.

And I said, "Look at them, Pop."

"I saw them," he said. "The whole back of the car's full of them."

Then I was holding P. O. M. tight, she feeling very small inside the quilted bigness of the dressing gown, and we were saying things to each other.

Then Karl came out and I said, "Hi, Karl."

"I'm so damned glad," he said. "They're marvellous."

M'Cola had the horns down by now and he and Kamau

were holding them so they could all see them in the light of the fire.

"What did you get?" I asked Karl.

"Just another one of those. What do you call them? Tendalla."

"Swell," I said. I knew I had one no one could beat and I hoped he had a good one too. "How big was he?"

"Oh, fifty-seven," Karl said.

"Let's see him," I said, cold in the pit of my stomach.

"He's over there," Pop said, and we went over. They were the biggest, widest, darkest, longest-curling, heaviest, most unbelievable pair of kudu horns in the world. Suddenly, poisoned with envy, I did not want to see mine again; never, never.

"That's great," I said, the words coming out as cheerfully as a croak. I tried it again. "That's swell. How did you get him?"

"There were three," Karl said. "They were all as big as that. I couldn't tell which was the biggest. We had a hell of a time. I hit him four or five times."

"He's a wonder," I said. I was getting so I could do it a little better but it would not fool anybody yet.

"I'm awfully glad you got yours," Karl said. "They're beauties. I want to hear all about them in the morning. I know you're tired tonight. Good night."

He went off, delicate as always, so we could talk about it if we wanted to.

"Come on over and have a drink," I called.

"No thanks, I think I better go to bed. I've got a sort of headache."

"Good night, Karl."

"Good night. Good night, Poor Old Mamma."

"Good night," we all said.

By the fire, with whiskey and soda, we talked and I told them about it all.

"Perhaps they'll find the bull," Pop said. "We'll offer a reward for the horns. Have them sent to the Game Department. How big is your biggest one?"

"Fifty-two."

"Over the curve?"

"Yes. Maybe he's a little better."

"Inches don't mean anything," Pop said. ."They're damned wonderful kudu."

"Sure. But why does he have to beat me so bloody badly?"

"He's got the luck," Pop said. "God, what a kudu. I've only seen one head killed over fifty in my life before. That was up on Kalal."

"We knew he had it when we left the other camp. The truck came in and told us," P. O. M. said. "I've spent all my time praying for you. Ask Mr. J. P."

"You'll never know what it meant to see that car come into the firelight with those damned horns sticking out," Pop said. "You old bastard."

"It's wonderful," P. O. M. said. "Let's go and look at them again."

"You can always remember how you shot them. That's what you really get out of it," Pop said. "They're damned wonderful kudu."

But I was bitter and I was bitter all night long. In the morning, though, it was gone. It was all gone and I have never had it again.

Pop and I were up and looking at the heads before breakfast. It was a gray, overcast morning and cold. The rains were coming.

"They're three marvellous kudu," he said.

"They look all right with the big one this morning," I said. They did, too, strangely enough. I had accepted the big one now and was happy to see him and that Karl had him. When you put them side by side they looked all right. They really did. They all were big.

"I'm glad you're feeling better," Pop said. "I'm feeling better myself."

"I'm really glad he has him," I said truly. "Mine'll hold me."

"We have very primitive emotions," he said. "It's impossible not to be competitive. Spoils everything, though."

"I'm all through with that," I said. "I'm all right again. I had quite a trip, you know."

"Did you not," said Pop.

"Pop, what does it mean when they shake hands and get hold of your thumb and pull it?"

"It's on the order of blood brotherhood but a little less formal. Who's been doing that to you?"

"Everybody but Kamau."

"You're getting to be a hell of a fellow," Pop said. "You must be an old timer out here. Tell me, are you much of a tracker and bird shot?"

"Go to hell."

"M'Cola has been doing that with you too?"

"Yes."

"Well, well," said Pop. "Let's get the little Memsahib and have some breakfast. Not that I'm feeling up to it."

"I am," I said. "I haven't eaten anything since day before yesterday."

"Drank some beer though, didn't you?"

"Ah, yes."

"Beer's a food," Pop said.

We got the little Memsahib and old Karl and had a very jolly breakfast.

A month later P. O. M., Karl, and Karl's wife who had come out and joined us at Haifa, were sitting in the sun against a stone wall by the Sea of Galilee eating some lunch and drinking a bottle of wine and watching the grebes out on the lake. The hills made shadows on the water, which was flat calm and rather stagnant looking. There were many grebes, making spreading wakes in the water as they swam, and I was counting them and wondering why they never were mentioned in the Bible. I decided that those people were not naturalists.

"I'm not going to walk on it," Karl said, looking out at the dreary lake. "It's been done already."

"You know," P. O. M. said, "I can't remember it. I can't remember Mr. J. P.'s face. And he's beautiful. I think about him and think about him and I can't see him. It's terrible. He isn't the way he looks in a photograph. In a little while I won't be able to remember him at all. Already I can't see him."

"You must remember him," Karl said to her.

"I can remember him," I said. "I'll write you a piece some time and put him in."